The Ostpolitik and Political Change in Germany

Edited by
Professor ROGER TILFORD

SAXON HOUSE | LEXINGTON BOOKS

Published by

SAXON HOUSE, D. C. Heath Ltd.
Westmead, Farnborough, Hants., England.

Jointly with

LEXINGTON BOOKS, D. C. Heath & Co.
Lexington, Mass. U.S.A.

ISBN 0 347 01073 3

Printed in Great Britain
by Unwin Brothers Limited
The Gresham Press, Old Woking, Surrey
A member of the Staples Printing Group

THE OSTPOLITIK AND POLITICAL CHANGE IN GERMANY

Contents

Editor's Note

This book originates from a conference entitled 'The Ostpolitik and the two Germanies', held at the University of Surrey in March 1974. Chapters 1, 2, 3 and 5 are based on papers delivered by the authors at that conference, though they have been modified to take account of subsequent developments, and have in some cases been expanded. Chapter 4 ('The Ostpolitik and Relations between the two Germanies') represents an addition to the original conference programme. Where a translation has been made from the German, it is, unless otherwise accredited, the author's own translation.

The gratitude of the editor and other contributors is due to the Universities Association of Contemporary European Studies, which sponsored the conference, assisted in its organisation and met the expenditure involved in tape-recording the conference proceedings and subsequently transcribing them.

Introduction

Roger TILFORD

Il n'y a que le provisoire qui dure

The assumption on which this book is based is that the *Ostpolitik* throws light on some of the major problems of political development in Germany, including those of national unity and identity, régime stability and legitimacy, style and patterns of political opposition, as well as the tradition of East–West dualism in German foreign alignments. It is clearly too early for firm conclusions to be drawn about the long-term implications of the *Ostpolitik* for many of these problems; but to the knowledgeable interpreter of the German scene the *Ostpolitik* has been accompanied and succeeded by indications of significant political change in Germany, and it is to these that the contributors to this volume turn their attention.

In this introduction some of the topics treated by the other contributors will be broached, without, it is hoped, trespassing too far onto their territory; in addition, a topic that has not been accorded a separate chapter, but which appears important – the *Ostpolitik* (and specifically the Basic Treaty between the two Germanies) as an illustration of the distinctive nature of German constitutionalism – is treated in some detail.

Adenauer's foreign policy, oriented to the West, was at first hotly disputed in the Federal Republic, primarily because the policy of integration with the West was seen to be at variance with the primary national goal of German foreign policy, as sanctified in the Constitution: the reunification of Germany. Until the second half of the 1950s, the SPD – then the chief opposition party – bitterly opposed Adenauer's foreign policy on the grounds that it would make the division of the nation permanent. Adenauer himself believed that it was in the United States and the Soviet Union that the key to the solution of the German problem was to be sought, but though he gained the verbal and paper support of the three Western powers for reunification, any solution acceptable to the Soviet Union would have meant West Germany's departure from the Western Alliance. Adenauer's policy of firmness towards Eastern Europe in effect strengthened the division of Germany. West German political overtures for reunification remained largely rhetorical, with West

Germany and its Western allies calling for free elections in Germany as a whole, and for the resultant German political entity to be free to choose its own alliances. The Soviet Union disseminated plans — distrusted in the West — for a military disengagement in Central Europe, and proposed co-operation of the two German states on a basis of parity in a German confederation; this proposal the Federal Republic could not accept, since it regarded itself as the sole legitimate government in Germany and steadfastly refused to recognise the German Democratic Republic as a sovereign and separate state. The standpoints of the two sides appeared irreconcilable.

But in West Germany the realisation slowly gained ground that Adenauer's policy of 'reunification through strength' (integration into the Western Alliance) did not tally with the facts. The military-strategic balance between East and West meant that no change in the German question was possible. Nevertheless, the West Germans continued to demand reunification and to claim revision of the Oder-Neisse frontier with Poland. They were thus the only ones who sought a change in the situation resulting from the Second World War, for both the Soviet Union and the United States and her allies had an interest in preserving the *status quo*. This led, during the 1960s, to West German fears that the super-powers would agree to a solution of the German question on the basis of the *status quo,* which would, in terms of West Germany's stated foreign policy goals, be at Germany's cost.

Adenauer's foreign policy was largely a product of the Cold War, and was at its most effective when East–West tension was at its sharpest. The more the tension eased, the more the premises of his foreign policy were undermined.

Such a relaxation of tension developed in the 1960s, and was followed by a change in West German foreign policy. The integration of the Federal Republic into Western alliances and organisations was not questioned, but an accommodation was sought with the East. The Erhard CDU/CSU government, and in particular Foreign Minister Schröder, made a start on this by facilitating closer economic relations with some East European countries. The Grand Coalition of the CDU/CSU and SPD intensified this policy and attempted to improve relations with Eastern Europe on the basis of the *status quo.* Diplomatic relations with Romania and Yugoslavia were established in 1967.

The new policy gathered pace at the beginning of the 1970s, and by 1973 the group of treaties that form the heart of the *Ostpolitik* — those with the Soviet Union, Poland and the German Democratic Republic — had been signed, as had the Berlin Agreement between the Western Allies and the Soviet Union. The details of these treaties are beyond the scope of this introduction which confines itself to the main points. The essence of the Federal Republic's treaty with the Soviet Union (confirmed by its treaty with Poland) was West German recognition of the Oder-Neisse Line as the frontier between East Germany and Poland, and agreement to negotiate an accord establishing formal relations with the German Democratic Republic. The Berlin Agreement is important in the development of West German *Ostpolitik* in that it directly affected relations between the two Germanies and was influenced strongly, on the Allies' side, by the Federal Republic. Its principal provisions were Soviet agreement to closer ties between West Berlin and West Germany, and recognition of the right of West Berliners to visit East Berlin and the GDR. In return, the Allies accepted the Soviet claim that West Berlin was not a constituent part of the Federal Republic. Finally as the climax of the *Ostpolitik* the Basic Treaty *(Grundvertrag)* between the two Germanies provided for the establishment of formal official relations between them, though the ruling of the West German Federal Constitutional Court on the constitutionality of this treaty is ambivalent (as will be seen later) and the West German government rejected the notion that the GDR constituted 'foreign' territory and withheld full diplomatic relations as normally provided under international law.

This complex of treaties and agreements has opened the way for improved West German relations with the countries of Eastern Europe and has furthered *détente* in Europe. A note of caution is appropriate here. One does not need to share the cynicism apparent in the French journalist André Fontaine's claim that *'détente* is Cold War by other means — and often the same means' - in remaining persuaded that there are many pitfalls in the path of continued *détente,* and in remaining sceptical — an attitude for which this book provides support — about claims that a 'convergence' of the political systems of East and West will accompany *détente.*

What is certain, however, is that the *Ostpolitik* has, for the time being at least, put an end to West Germany's questioning of the *status quo* in Central Europe. The situation created at the end of the Second World War has been accepted, and the traditional view of reunification — with reservations on the part of the Federal Constitutional Court — dropped.

The *Ostpolitik* has also resulted in the dropping of the Hallstein Doctrine, one of the pillars of Adenauer's foreign policy. The Hallstein Doctrine was rooted in the Federal Republic's claim to have the only legitimate (freely elected, democratic) German Government and to speak not only for itself but for all Germans. The doctrine aimed — until 1967, for the most part successfully — at preventing third countries from simultaneously entertaining diplomatic relations both with the GDR and with the Federal Republic. It was a major barrier to East Germany's attempts to win increased international recognition.

For a long time, the official policy of the Federal Republic denied that the German Democratic Republic was a state at all; it was designated as the 'Soviet-occupied zone' or the 'so-called German Democratic Republic' or the 'German Democratic Republic' (in quotation marks). For a long time, too, official policy was aimed at isolating the GDR internationally. Until the mid-1960s, reunification was understood by *both* governments essentially as the annexation of one part of the country by the other. Only since that time has this view changed. Admittedly, Adenauer attempted in 1955 to create better conditions for reunification by establishing diplomatic relations with Moscow — the first breach of the Hallstein Doctrine — but nothing much came of it.

The slogans and rhetoric of West German foreign policy under Adenauer became increasingly empty after 1965. A new beginning was called for. Chancellor Brandt chose the way of voluntarily recognising the *status quo*. The *Ostpolitik* heralded the end of claims to German unity based on the Wilhelmine national state. A revision of the Oder-Neisse Line now also seems beyond the realms of possibility. In addition, it may be argued that the belief in one German nation is obsolete — though here one should remember that official political language in the Federal Republic speaks of 'two German states of one nation'.

The man to whose dynamic diplomatic activity the *Ostpolitik* owes most, Willy Brandt, has resigned as West German Chancellor. His opponents in West Germany have claimed — not convincingly — that his resignation implies an admission that the *Ostpolitik* was ill-conceived. Relations between the two Germanies are still very strained and riven by suspicion, despite the Basic Treaty. Brandt's successor, Helmut Schmidt, was thought by some to be a less enthusiastic adherent of the *Ostpolitik* than his forerunner. Nothing that has happened so far indicates that this is true, even if Schmidt does give expression to the continuing difficulties of inter-German relations more readily than Brandt. Explaining his standpoint in August 1974, Schmidt maintained that it was in the interest both of the Federal Republic and the GDR to stay in line with global political tendencies and not to isolate themselves. Despite 'many predictable threats . . . and setbacks, relations between the two German states will in the foreseeable future move ever further away from the situation which reached its climax in the late Fifties and early Sixties [with the building of the Berlin Wall]'.[1]

In this sketch of the development of West German policy towards the countries of Eastern Europe, certain changes in West Germany's relations with those countries and with the GDR have already been indicated. In foreign policy, the more fluid situation, which is both a cause and a consequence of the *Ostpolitik*, has, for some, revived memories of an earlier East—West dualism in Germany's foreign alignments. The Rapallo Treaty (1922), which involved playing off the East against the West, is perhaps the most vivid symbol of this dualism. Has the *Ostpolitik* created a situation in which the 'spirit of Rapallo' can survive? This is one of the chief concerns of Roger Morgan in Chapter 5.

It is, however, with the domestic politics of the two Germanies that much of this book is concerned. The Federal Republic has outlived the presupposition on which it was founded; the provisional state has achieved permanence. A new and, in some ways, still fragile liberal democracy was confronted with a policy, the *Ostpolitik*, which plucked at the sensitive nerve of national identity and questioned some of the premises of its foundation. The policy was carried through shortly after the Federal Republic had undergone the crucial test of any new parliamentary régime — its first change of governing party; and the party chiefly responsible for implementing the policy — the Social Democratic Party — was one whose national loyalty was historically suspect in the eyes of many Germans, who also remembered its earlier Marxist affiliations. What are the implications of these factors for democratic politics in the Federal Republic? And what implications does the achievement of recognition, both internationally and by the Federal Republic, have for the domestic political climate in the GDR? These are the questions pursued throughout this book.

In particular, the link between *Ostpolitik,* national identity and the legitimacy of the two régimes is explored. The notions of legitimacy and national identity are central to the analysis of the stability of political systems. For the student of politics too they are difficult nettles to grasp: they are scarcely amenable to quantitative measurement and cannot be used as precisely as is perhaps desirable. However, to ignore them would be to fail to ask interesting and significant questions, and, possibly, to indulge in an emasculated analysis.

It is scarcely surprising that West Germans should handle such concepts as 'nation', 'national identity' and 'national consciousness' with extreme care. Largely taken for granted among the Federal Republic's West European neighbours, such phenomena, and their discussion, have been cast into shadow in Germany by the extreme nationalism, culminating in the excess of the Nazi era, that has characterised much of its political development for the last century.

Allegiance to a democratic political régime stands in a vexed relationship to the problem of national unity in Germany. From the point of view of the ideological, economic and social requisites of a stable liberal democracy, Bonn is far better off than was Weimar, at the time of that experiment in liberal democracy. However, the replacement of the profound ideological divisions and confusion of Weimar Germany (which, for all its drawbacks, was *one* Germany) with a Germany clearly divided into *two* states, embodying distinct ideologies and incorporated into opposing ideological camps, has revived the debate about the notions of 'state' and 'nation' and that vexed relationship between them that many historians consider to be at the root of German political aberration. By this they usually mean divergence from the liberal democractic political development of the English-speaking countries and some of Germany's West European neighbours. The concepts of the nation-state and of democracy, instead of growing side by side and supporting each other, grew apart in the course of the nineteenth century, and in the twentieth century have often appeared to be mutually exclusive. The nation came to be seen as something rooted in ascribed cultural qualities such as language – hence the term *Kulturnation* – and therefore as something exclusive of the development of a set of political and social values transcending national loyalty and grandeur, such as those of representative democracy and personal liberties. Indeed, the latter were rejected, particularly during the life of the Weimar Republic, as being *un*German. The 'nation' and 'democracy', it seemed, could not coexist in Germany.

Until recently, the division of Germany resulting from the Second World War seemed a particularly vivid illustration of the historical conflict in Germany of these two main fruits of the French Revolution. What were West Germans to prefer: democracy or national unity? Should they be prepared to sacrifice liberal democracy, or at least accept a dilution of it, in the interests of national unity (reunification), or ought they be prepared to sacrifice national unity in the interests of the maintenance of liberal democracy in at least the western part of Germany? The late Karl Jaspers,[2] for one, was in no doubt that this was the essential long-term choice that faced West Germany, and insisted that democracy should be given preference over national unity. However, the dilemma formulated so passionately by Jaspers has been resolved – with apparent finality – by the *Ostpolitik*. West Germany has, at least for the time being, turned its back on national unity, as epitomised by the Bismarckian nation-state, and the form of nationalism associated with it. Jaspers' spectre of West German democracy being subverted by a lingering nostalgia for national unity has, it seems, been exorcised. But does not a sense of shared identity remain an invaluable, possibly indispensable, support for a new and fragile régime, especially where this régime does not possess deep roots in the political culture of the country concerned? An important premise of William Paterson's investigation of the relationship between *Ostpolitik* and régime stability in West Germany (Chapter 1) is that the legitimacy of a régime — or the extent to which it is excepted by the people that live under its jurisdiction — is closely related to the existence of a sense of national identity on the part of those people. Have the conditions been created — in part by the *Ostpolitik* — for the emergence of a specifically *West* German sense of national identity, untrammelled by the ballast of earlier German nationalism and linked to the universal political ideals of democracy and liberty? Has the historical dichotomy of 'state' and 'nation', or rather 'democratic state' and 'nation', been resolved?

The barriers to the emergence of a West German national identity should not be underestimated. As has already been pointed out, the perversion of the idea of 'nation' by the Nazis, and the national disgrace that followed, have cast a shadow on the nation concept and all it stands for, inhibiting the development of affective links — which is what national pride in a country's political institutions amounts to — between the West German régime and its citizens. To call for even this type of West German national consciousness is, in West Germany, to risk being labelled 'incorrigible'. Nor should one underestimate, moreover, the resistance of Germans who had their 'fingers burned' during the Nazi era to anything smacking of the cult of the irrational that flourished in the 1920s[3] or of the blatantly irrational appeal of the Nazis. The result is a tendency to avoid even that degree of affective political behaviour that, expressed in terms of pride in national institutions such as the monarchy or presidency, is taken for granted in Britain or the United States. However, the Nazi régime collapsed thirty years ago. Since the middle 1960s the inhibitions and taboos that characterised the post-war period have been dropping away, to be replaced by a normalisation of political behaviour. The *Ostpolitik* itself may be seen as one expression of this; the emergence of affective links to the West German régime, facilitated in part by the *Ostpolitik*, may prove to be another (see Chapter 1).

Not only a shared sense of identity, but also, closely linked, a shared sense of history, a common view of the German past, is considered by some to be an essential support of the liberal-democratic régime in West Germany.[4] However, as has frequently been pointed out, the Federal Republic lacks this sense of history, even though its inception was an explicit reaction against Nazism and much that preceded it. Complaints about the failure to 'come to terms with the past' (*'Bewältigung der*

Vergangenheit') have been frequent. This failure was bolstered by government policies that seemed to ignore the practical results of the Second World War — the Federal government insisting on reunification as a 'constitutional imperative', claiming itself to be the sole legitimate representative of all Germans, refusing to recognise the Oder-Neisse Line, and insisting on the validity of Germany's 1937 borders — and by the anti-Communist and anti-Slav ideology inculcated by the Nazis and subsequently sanctioned by the Cold War situation.

One reason for the lack of fruitful introspection about the recent past, suggests the psychologist Alexander Mitscherlich,[5] was the suppression of the conscious memory of that period. This mass psychological device — termed by him 'the inability to mourn' — was a means for coping with a degree of guilt that, if fully admitted, might have been too much to bear. The result was emotional paralysis as regards the Nazi period and, consequently, a lack of spontaneity in coming to terms with it. Despite reservations about Mitscherlich's method (his generalisations about social-psychological phenomena are based on psychological case-studies of individuals) his analysis seems to many students of contemporary Germany to explain a great deal.

The normalisation of political behaviour since 1965 has probably helped to change this mood, and it can be persuasively argued that the *Ostpolitik* accelerated the change. The policy props supporting the taboo on full recognition of responsibility for the Nazi past were removed: the Oder-Neisse Line and the GDR were recognised. No longer could whole areas of policy be conducted as if the Second World War had not happened: realities had to be faced. Vividly symbolic of this change — and peculiarly appropriate as a way of overcoming the 'inability to mourn' — was Brandt's spontaneous gesture of kneeling before the memorial to the victims of Nazi tyranny in Poland. This, for the German populace, was the most cathartic moment of the *Ostpolitik.*

Despite the fact that a lack of historical awareness — assisted, perhaps, by the recurrence of abrupt breaks in the continuity of German history — remains one of the most striking characteristics of West Germans generally, and the young in particular, the *Ostpolitik* would appear to have made it possible for West Germans to develop a shared interpretation of recent German history, an interpretation congruent with the origins and norms of the new constitutional order in West Germany.

Both Germanies are confronted with the same problem. Economic consolidation has been achieved, and now the stabilisation of their respective political systems requires that political legitimacy be achieved as well. In West, as in East, Germany, the problem of creating an image both of its own and of the other system — together with the process of self-examination that this entails — is a foremost concern. Élites in both countries are deeply concerned with defining 'state' and 'nation' and with drawing lines of demarcation and delimitation.[6]

The East German attempt to underpin the legitimacy of the régime of the Socialist Unity Party (SED) by putting forward an idea of the nation limited to 'their' Germans must be seen in this context. In the official ideology of the German Democratic Republic, the concept of the nation is connected with Marxist class theory: the GDR is seen as comprising a new type of nation, the 'Socialist nation'. This view, which limits the nation to a social class, is thus exclusive and as such, has surprising affinities with the traditional German concept of the *Kulturnation.* In addition, the East German régime has been quick to enlist a highly selective version of German history as a further aid to legitimacy.

The chief objective of West Germany's *Ostpolitik,* notwithstanding its implications for West German domestic politics, was the solution of international problems, including relations between the two Germanies. In contrast, the GDR's foreign policy was in Peter Ludz's view, aimed mainly at stabilising the SED régime.[7] The fact that foreign policy has, in the GDR a greater bearing on the domestic political situation than is usual in industrialised countries, is perhaps indicated by the amount of attention devoted to it in the East German mass media.

The relative instability of the East German régime is, according to Ludz, indicated in two main ways:

(i) by the need for security, as reflected in *Abgrenzung* (demarcation), which began in autumn 1970 and involved the intensified ideological schooling and political control of the SED cadres (see Chapter 3);
(ii) by the party's reluctance to facilitate, let alone encourage, popular identification with the political system of the GDR.

As regards (i), it is possible that *Abgrenzung* has reached its peak. The SED, it seems, has succeeded in disciplining its cadres and has realised that to go too far in ensuring loyalty may adversely affect its international prestige, about which it is very sensitive. It has therefore become more cautious. In addition, the SED is seeking to avoid undermining the confidence in its desire for *détente* that its response to *Ostpolitik* has engendered.

With respect to (ii), the SED feels, in Ludz's view, that more political spontaneity, participation, and pluralism could — even if limited to the present politically active groups — set in motion forces that would be difficult for the party to control. The officially proclaimed 'openness' of the Youth Festival of 1973 did not really belie this. After the festival many young East Germans must have been conscious of the return to grim ideological smugness and isolation.

Ludz sees the SED régime as characterised by a 'legitimacy deficit'. Economic stabilisation has been achieved, but political legitimacy is some way off. The attitude to the régime is one of passiveness and resignation. He goes on to argue that the 'legitimacy deficit' has assumed new virulence since the Basic Treaty opened up the GDR for millions of visitors from the Federal Republic. For citizens of the GDR, 'demarcation' from, and competition with, West Germany renders the question of legitimacy and an independent identity acute. Conditions in the two countries, including the implementation of basic individual rights, are compared. This is confirmed, Ludz maintains, by countless reports from the GDR.

A related consequence of the *Ostpolitik* for the GDR is that its representatives now people the international scene. The SED régime is seen by some, perhaps unjustly, as the true German successor to the Nazi régime — an attitude exemplified by the representatives of Israel in the United Nations. They indicated that they would raise the question of conditions in the GDR as soon as that country acceded to the UN. They did not; but the threat remains. To this extent, argues Ludz, the 'legitimacy deficit' of the East German political leadership has become more manifest in the wake of the *Ostpolitik* and the ensuing recognition of the GDR by foreign countries. Paradoxically, the GDR's promotion to the international stage opens the way — precisely because more attention is focused on it — for new threats to the stability of the SED régime. Ludz's interpretation is authoritative and stimulating, but it seems a little contrived and should be set alongside that of David Childs (Chapter 3), who sees the stability of the régime as resting on surer ground.

In West Germany, in contrast to the GDR, the 'nation' is still officially held to denote the shared history for which *all* Germans are responsible. This view has survived the *Ostpolitik* and is neatly summed up in Brandt's phrase 'two states of one nation'. It argues that personal relationships and shared language and culture still provide a basis for a pan-German national existence. Adherence to this 'one nation' thesis at the official level is, it can be argued, at odds with the intrinsic thrust of the *Ostpolitik*, which, by recognising the GDR, helps create the possibility, as William Paterson argues, of the emergence of a specifically West German sense of identity. Public opinion surveys in the Federal Republic have for some time indicated that the West German populace regard the German Democratic Republic in much the same way as they regard Austria.

10

Popular sentiment, at any rate, does not seem to support the 'one nation' thesis.

Here official West German policy is less consistent ideologically than its East German counterpart (though it may be more faithful to German history); the 'nation' is not officially recruited in support of the West German polity in the way that the East Germans call it up in the service of Marxist class theory. However, Brandt had domestic opposition to the *Ostpolitik* to consider, and the Federal Constitutional Court's reservations about the extent to which the Basic Treaty with the GDR was consistent with the 'reunification imperative' contained in the Basic Law may have been foreseen. Both these considerations may have played a part in his continued insistence on the 'one-nation' thesis, overtaken though it may have been by events and changed attitudes.

It was important for political integration in the Federal Republic that the *Ostpolitik* was carried out by a government led by the Social Democrats. In Germany, the concept of the 'nation' has been historically associated with the Right. The Left was frequently excluded, regarded by large sections of the population as 'unpatriotic' (the Kaiser called the Social Democrats 'rogues without a fatherland') and 'subversive', the primary allegiance of Marxists, including a large part of the labour movement in both the trade unions and the SPD, being to the international working class. This contributed to one of the major rifts in German society, vividly illustrated in the case of the Weimar Republic. Here it prevented the emergence of a national consensus in favour of the régime, which was regarded by its opponents as having 'sold out' German interests by recognising as valid the Treaty of Versailles. These opponents were labelled the *nationale Opposition,* implying that they were the true guardians of the 'nation'.

In the Federal Republic, the Marxist past of the SPD was shrugged off as long ago as 1959, with the publication of the Godesberg programme. However, some of the rhetoric employed by opponents of the *Ostpolitik* — the term *Anerkennungspartei* (recognition party), for instance, which was used after the First World War to berate the SPD-led government for recognising the validity of the Treaty of Versailles — was a reminder that a few, at any rate, still harboured suspicions about the 'national' reliability of the SPD. Nevertheless, the SPD-inspired *Ostpolitik,* which both recognised (albeit belatedly) that West Germany had a price to pay for the Second World War, and accepted a truncated Germany, has been widely approved by the West German population (as was clearly shown by the 1972 election) and chalked up to the SPD as a positive achievement. This fact provides evidence (not accepted by all) that the last vestiges of this suspicion of the SPD are disappearing, and that a historical rift representing a threat to the legitimacy of the régime has finally been removed. It is also, of course, another indication of the extent to which popular pan-German sentiment has waned.

The existence of a 'loyal' political opposition seen as having a positive value in the workings of government is often cited as a hallmark of democratic societies.[8] German political development has in the past been hostile to the emergence of such an opposition. A number of illiberal traditions subsumed by Dahrendorf under the label of 'the longing for synthesis'[9] and claimed by him to be influential still, have hindered the articulation of divergent political opinions and interests, and consequently the functioning of a 'loyal' opposition. Such traditions include the Hegelian 'above-party' approach to politics, the plebiscitary democratic tradition,[10] and the propensity for putting *das Nationale* before *das Soziale*. Earlier German development was typified by an 'opposition of principle',[11] opposition not to a policy but to the political system or form of government as such; again, the Weimar Republic, where the political system was under fire from parties of both the extreme Left and the extreme Right, is a case in point.

Nor, returning to the Federal Republic, should the extent to which the division of Germany has inhibited political debate, choice and opposition in West Germany (not to mention East Germany) be underestimated. In a divided Germany, opposition, in the shape of permanent, and often unreasonable, criticism of West German policies, institutions and public figures, has come from the arch- (but German) enemy in the German Democratic Republic. This has often led to the devaluation of criticism emanating from sources within the Federal Republic itself, any criticism that resembles that coming from the other side of the border being viewed with particular distrust. The fact that two hostile systems exist side by side on German soil has tended to pervert all opposition into opposition to the other system, and to deprive domestic conflicts of political expression.

The ideological, social and economic prerequisites of a viable pluralistic democracy are present to a far greater degree in the Federal Republic than they were in the Weimar Republic, and it is likely that the antipluralistic traditions of which Dahrendorf complained have further waned since 1965, when his remarks were published. Nevertheless, the *Ostpolitik* remained a stiff test, both for the stability of the relatively new parliamentary régime and for the quality of the opposition; all the more so as the Federal Republic had only a short time before undergone its first change of leading governing party (and therefore of leading opposition

12

party). The *Ostpolitik* touched on the sensitive nerve of national unity and was potentially highly divisive. It represented a test of régime stability and of 'loyal' opposition similar to that failed by both the Weimar Republic (over the lost Eastern territories) and the Fifth French Republic (over Algeria). It may have had the support of the large majority of the population, but there was a sharp polarisation of opinion within the Bundestag. However, despite these difficulties, there was no threat to the proper functioning of the democratic régime, and the Christian Democrats, while exhibiting a continued tendency to 'fundamentalist' opposition (described by Geoffrey Pridham in Chapter 2), behaved by and large as a 'responsible' opposition. In this respect it can be said that the challenge posed by the *Ostpolitik* was overcome. The stability of the régime was convincingly demonstrated.

Not only was the polarisation that characterised debates on the *Ostpolitik* in the sixth Bundestag (1969–72) not fundamentally divisive, but it also made a significant contribution to political integration. This at least is the view held by Robert Leicht. [12] Whereas, in the Weimar Republic, it was the parties of the extreme Right and Left who were responsible for the polarisation of the Reichstag, with the parties of the Centre being the ones to suffer, in the sixth Bundestag the polarisation emanated from the parties of the Centre, who contested the middle ground of the electorate. This tended to be disguised by the clamour of political polemic. The *aim* of the polemic was to depict the other party as radical and hence unacceptable to the middle-ground and undecided voters. Its *effect* was to attract marginal voters of the Right and Left to the large parties of the Centre (and, incidentally, to leave the voters in the middle ground, who were in the main already persuaded of the inevitability of changes in Bonn's Eastern policies, rather unimpressed). This parliamentary polarisation over a fundamental and controversial issue thus had the opposite effect to that predicted by Cassandras haunted by the spectre of Weimar; far from causing a rift in the parliamentary system, it was actually a force for political integration. [13] In a sense the polarisation was not merely a result of the clash over the *Ostpolitik;* it was also an instrument helping that policy succeed. This gives further evidence both of the existence of a broad consensus on the rules of the political game, and of the ability to tolerate a sharp degree of conflict while keeping within the framework of those rules.

Viewing the relationship between the *Ostpolitik* and political change in the Federal Republic as an account, the balance has so far been positive. However, some West German scholars, not all of whom opposed the *Ostpolitik,* are pessimistic about its consequences for the West German political scene. They point to the re-emergence since 1967 of a radical, if splintered, Left, and argue that the commitment of the 'new' Left (which lies partly within and partly outside the SPD) to liberal democracy is open to serious doubt. The *Ostpolitik*, for such critics, has resulted in a completely new situation: it has unwittingly established the preconditions for the emergence — admittedly not in the near future — of a Popular Front spanning the two Germanies. [14] Notwithstanding that the criticism of the GDR by most groups on the far Left is no less vehement than their criticism of the Federal Republic, the *Ostpolitik* and the recognition of the GDR is held to have increased West German receptiveness to the ideas of East German Communism. In particular, the temptation of a tactical co-operation between the extreme Left in the Federal Republic and the SED régime has, it is alleged, been increased. [15]

Admittedly, in contrast to Italy and France, Germany possesses a ruling Communist Party: the SED in the German Democratic Republic. However, unlike their fellows in Italy and France, the Marxist Left in West Germany is numerically insignificant in the population at large and enjoys scant support among workers; it is restricted virtually to the educational system, in particular the universities (its importance *there* should not be underestimated). In view of this, the anxiety of Hans-Peter Schwarz [16] and others that the SPD is faced with a choice between a union of Socialists spanning the German border and the solidarity of non-Marxist Social Democrats within the Federal Republic may seem a trifle overwrought. The Jusos (Young Socialists) and other groups are certainly unruly, inconvenient for the SPD, and susceptible to political *Schwärmerei;* but there is little evidence outside the universities, of a major ideological rift in the Left, even if a radicalisation in the event of a serious economic recession should not be discounted. Nor is there any real evidence at present that the increased contact, between East and West Germans, and the recognition (and increased respectability) afforded to the GDR as a result of the *Ostpolitik,* have strengthened the possibility of ideological subversion of West Germany by East Germany. The *Ostpolitik* may be *related* to the emergence of the 'new' Left — they are both expressions of the political normalisation referred to earlier — but it did not *cause* it. The GDR's clandestine support for potentially disruptive groups in the Federal Republic long predates the *Ostpolitik,* as does the ability of such groups to turn to the GDR for help.

The way in which the *Ostpolitik* was contested in domestic West German politics throws light on an important aspect of German political tradition. It is an illuminating case study in the 'legalistic approach to politics', which is a distinctive characteristic of German constitutionalism

14

and, indeed, of German political culture altogether.[17] This is the tendency to seek legal answers (with — at least in a country with a codified law — their aura of infallibility and absolute objectivity) to questions that are highly political and to which, therefore, there is rarely *one* answer valid for all time.

The tradition of the legalistic approach to politics contributes to the 'longing for synthesis', which, as we have seen, Dahrendorf saw as characteristic of German society and as fundamentally illiberal, since it encourages the avoidance of legitimate conflict and thus deprives society of the dynamic and potentially beneficial consequences of conflict articulated in agreement with agreed rules.

The existence of a constitutional court can be argued to promote a legalistic approach to politics, especially where the tradition of 'judicial self-restraint' in highly political questions (such as is practised by the American Supreme Court) is not developed. This risk is all the greater in a country, like Germany, where the German version of the 'Rule of Law', the *Rechtsstaat,* was established prior to the introduction of parliamentary government and has not traditionally embraced the notion of parliamentary sovereignty.

It was perhaps inevitable that the new régime in West Germany, having no deep roots in popular support, would enlist the support of a legal tradition, whose high standing in Germany had, rightly or wrongly, not been greatly impaired by its implication in the Nazi atrocities. Nor is it surprising, after the lawlessness of the Nazi régime, that the earlier positivist legal tradition should have reasserted itself, although the tendency of this tradition to insist on the letter, rather than the spirit, of the law, may in a sense be considered to have helped the Nazi seizure of power. However, the approach to political conflict implicit in this tradition, especially in a country characterised by a *Juristenmonopol* [18] (the quasi-monopoly of positions in the political élites by those with legal training) is seen by many as a continuing barrier to the legitimacy of the parliamentary system.

Where does the *Ostpolitik* fit into this? West German foreign policy has from the beginning been built around legal or quasi-legal doctrine, as the terminology of some of the main tenets of this policy illustrate: the *Alleinvertretungsrecht* (the *right* to represent all Germans); the *Selbstbestimmungsrecht* (the *right* to determine the sort of political order you wish to live under); the *Recht auf Heimat* (the *right* of expelled Germans to their homelands in Eastern Europe); and the Hallstein *Doctrine.* In the early years of the Federal Republic, this formulation of foreign policy in terms of legal dogma tended to place strict limits on the

15

flexibility and room to manoeuvre that most foreign-policy makers seek.

The stated objective of Adenauer's foreign policy — German reunification — was written into the Basic Law. According to the Preamble to the Basic Law 'the German people', who enacted the constitution, 'have also acted on behalf of those Germans to whom participation was denied. The entire German people are called upon to achieve in free self-determination the unity and freedom of Germany.[19] The Federal Constitutional Court, in its 1955 ruling outlawing the Communist Party in West Germany, stated that the 'Preamble to the Basic Law has . . . political significance. But beyond that it contains legal implications . . . From the Preamble is to be derived the *legal obligation,*[20] incumbent on all the political organs of state of the Federal Republic, to strive for the unity of Germany with every means available.'[21] This ruling has been interpreted as a constitutional taboo on the renunciation of reunification.

In 1973, the government of Bavaria and the Bavarian Christian-Social Union, the governing party, lodged a complaint with the Federal Constitutional Court to the effect that the Basic Treaty between West and East Germany was unconstitutional on the grounds that it was incompatible with the 'reunification imperative' contained in the Preamble to the Basic Law. The Court decided that the Basic Treaty was constitutional, *but only in the sense outlined in the ruling that accompanied the decision.* This ruling stated, 'It must be clear that present conditions at the border between West and East Germany — the Berlin Wall, barbed wire, death-strips, orders to shoot — are incompatible with the treaty. To this extent the treaty provides grounds in law for the Federal government to do everything within its power to change and do away with these inhuman conditions.'[22]

Here it must be said that, regrettable as some of the practices at the border may be, no dispassionate analyst of the political scene in Central Europe would deny that the border between the two Germanies, far from being incompatible with the Basic Treaty, is one of its prerequisities. So long as the stability of the GDR cannot be achieved in more acceptable ways, the border is accepted in both East and West (whether openly or not) as a means of stabilising the situation in Central Europe. In short, acceptance of the Basic Treaty implies acceptance of the border and its political function.[23]

However, this political finding cannot be formulated in constitutional law terms. The judges could not have said, as the politicians did, that the border and the treaty 'were incompatible in the long term'. According to the rules of legal interpretation this would have meant, 'Now and for a certain time the behaviour practised at the border is compatible with the

16

Basic Treaty.' To give, in this way, legal sanction to this behaviour — East German border-guards have orders to shoot — is unthinkable. This whole episode vividly demonstrates that there are inevitably vital political considerations that cannot be formulated in legal categories. It also points to a clash and inconsistency between West German national law on the one hand, and the Federal Republic's international law position and international interests on the other.[24]

A similar inconsistency exists over the status of Berlin. The Federal Constitutional Court insists on the view that West Berlin is part of the Federal Republic subject to certain limitations by the three Western powers.[25] However, the Four-Power Agreement on Berlin — to the conclusion of which, in September 1971, the West German government made a direct contribution — reiterates the standpoint of the Four Powers on the subject: West Berlin is *not* a constituent part of the Federal Republic, although relations between West Berlin and the Federal Republic may be cultivated as long as Berlin's status is not infringed. The Constitutional Court's interpretation was thus at variance with the Berlin Agreement, which formed an important stage in the progress of the *Ostpolitik*.

There are other examples. The supplementary agreements provided for by the Basic Treaty may not, in the view of the Federal Constitutional Court, 'contain any infringement or relaxation of the secrecy of the postal and telecommunications services for Germans in either West or East Germany, nor any limitation of the free exchange of opinion and information.'[26] The Federal Constitutional Court appears to be attempting here to extend the basic rights that the West German constitution accords to West German citizens, to citizens of the GDR, as well as in a sense prolonging the 'right to represent all Germans' that it was the purpose of the Basic Treaty to end once and for all. Simply by concluding agreements with the GDR, the Federal Republic cannot hope to extend its constitutional embrace to citizens of that country. The view of the court just quoted would mean that no agreement with the GDR would be possible without its having been previously converted to the West German constitution — clearly an unrealistic expectation. This in turn would mean that the Federal Republic would under no circumstance recognise the GDR as a sovereign state, since the basic rights outlined in the West German constitution are violated there. However, it was precisely that recognition of the GDR that was the aim and result of the *Ostpolitik*.[27]

The Constitutional Court's view that the border between the two Germanies is of the same kind as the borders between the *Länder* of the

Federal Republic does not merit discussion here. It could be valid only if the GDR were a component *Land* (province) of the Federal Republic.

As we have seen, the court decided that the Basic Treaty was constitutional, but the ruling accompanying that decision undermines it in such a way that it is difficult to understand how the judges could have reached the decision in the first place. The answer, one supposes, is that the judges were, on the one hand, impressed by the paramount political importance of the Basic Treaty (and by the serious political consequences − on both the domestic and the international fronts − of a declaration of unconstitutionality), but that they were, on the other hand, unable to reconcile it with constitutional precedent, i.e. the legally binding interpretation given to the policy of reunification in the Constitutional Court's 1955 ruling on the Communist Party.

The tendency to attempt to force political circumstances of a highly complex and ambivalent nature into a framework of unambiguous legal dogma is rooted in a legalistic mentality, and so, it may be claimed, is the propensity to elevate tenets of national law to the status of legal claims between states.

Reunification as a 'constitutional imperative' is a reflection of Adenauer's policy of 'reunification through strength' (military domination). It has long been realised that a 'policy of strength' has no prospect of success where reunification is concerned. It is therefore a matter for concern that West Germany's highest court has elevated a political objective that is attainable only from a position of military dominance to an immutable legal obligation.

But, it may be objected, the reservations of the Federal Constitutional Court have been overtaken by events: the Basic Treaty was, after all, ratified; it was, despite everything, declared to be constitutional; and it was the only aspect of the *Ostpolitik* to come before the court, for neither the treaty with the Soviet Union, nor that with Poland, did. However, not only the decision, but also the ruling − i.e. the reservations − of the court are regarded as having a standing in law, as setting constitutional precedent. Precedent and support have been created for the contestants in *future* political and legal battles in West Germany.

To understand the significance of this it will be necessary to turn briefly to another aspect of German constitutionalism: the tendency to regard the constitution not only as a set of procedural rules, but also as a sort of 'secular plan for salvation', [28] enjoying the status almost of a sacred commandment. [29] The word shall become flesh, as it were. Political reality must be made to conform to the constitution. In this vein the constitution is regarded as an inventory of legitimate political phenomena.

18

Political phenomena not listed in the constitution — political parties in the Weimar Republic, interest groups in the Federal Republic — may be considered to be lacking in legitimacy, especially if they are contradicted by something that *is*, such as the principle of reunification. Where this tradition obtains, and especially where the constitution ventures beyond procedural into substantive law — i.e. prescribes actual policies (such as reunification) — the inevitable and potentially fruitful gap between the constitution and political reality is likely to be construed as a problem, as a weakness to be overcome.

In the fact that the inevitable tension between the norm and the reality of political life is felt to be so oppressive is concealed one of the chief traditional threats to politics in Germany. [30] One consequence of this approach is the tendency — more deeply rooted in Germany than in the English-speaking countries — to see politics as an ugly, dirty business. One symptom is the tendency of German public and constitutional lawyers, as well as many political scientists, to see the divergence between the constitution and political reality as *the* major theme of public and constitutional law. The enormous literature [31] elaborating this theme is evidence of this. The polemic, characteristic of this literature, about the allegedly intolerable discrepancy between the norm and political reality also constitutes 'the lowest common denominator of all criticism levelled at politics in the Federal Republic' (Hennis). Not the least assiduous exponents of this constitutional tradition in recent years have been the radical democrats, the utopian 'democratisers', who have sought — and found — in the constitution vindication of their vision of a 'concretised' democracy (the extension of the principles and procedures of parliamentary democracy to other spheres, such as universities and schools. The claim of one Left-wing writer, Hans-Magnus Enzensberger, that the 'Basic Law is a promise to be redeemed by revolution' [32] is significant here. In the context of this tradition, the ambivalence of the Constitutional Court's decision and ruling on the Basic Treaty may be seen to assume new importance.

The dangers of taking a constitution too literally, and of incorporating in it substantive law, are illustrated by another topical case, the *numerus clausus* [33] issue at the universities. According to Article 12 of the Basic Law, all Germans have the right to choose freely their place of education. A strict interpretation of this would render the *numerus clausus* unconstitutional. However, the Constitutional Court contented itself with asserting that the *numerus clausus* lay 'at the limits of what was constitutionally acceptable'. It is difficult to see what else it could have done. Can political claims be made without at the same time saying how the claims are to be implemented, without taking into account the financial resources available, and without deciding which of the competing claims on those resources have priority? The Constitutional Court is competent to do none of those things, but, as a result of pressures in the West German constitutional system, found itself in a situation where it had either to underpin a constitutional guarantee or to reach a decision that weakened that guarantee, thereby taking the risk of undermining its own authority. It wisely chose the latter, but should the dilemma have arisen? The substantive constitution is secure against abuse only in a political culture that recognises and articulates political conflict freely and openly, that does not rely on a regressive legalism to secure freedom and social justice, but rather sees in political conflict a means to political integration. [34] However, in such a political culture a substantive constitution would be redundant.

The substantive constitution is possibly an expression of an overriding desire for integration. But attempts to create a kind of 'pre-stabilised harmony' (reminiscent of Dahrendorf's 'longing for synthesis') by trying to codify, in constitutional law, decisions that can only ever emerge from the continuing clash of divergent political opinions are problematic. The legal codification of substantive political objectives implies that these objectives no longer have to be striven for politically, but simply claimed under the law. In the context of German constitutional tradition, the substantive constitution introduces to political discussion a distinctly unpolitical outlook. [35]

In many ways, as this book demonstrates, the *Ostpolitik* may be seen to have increased the legitimacy of West German democracy. However, the invocation of the Constitutional Court, an allegedly impartial agency, illustrates how a facet of traditional German political culture continues to exert influence and acts a barrier to such legitimacy.

The impartiality of the Federal Constitutional Court may be illusory anyway. One of its members was barred from participating in the Basic Treaty case because his impartiality was in doubt. The judges' vote on the treaty was four in favour to three against. The judges are elected by the Bundesrat and a committee of the Bundestag. Moreover, the election of new judges that was due in April 1971 was delayed until the autumn of that year, because the political parties, already aware that the Basic Treaty might be taken to court, were haggling behind the scenes about the new appointments.

When highly political decisions are removed from parliament to the jurisdiction of the courts they are deprived of the legitimising control and sanction of parliament and the electorate. A politically dysfunctional and

20

disintegrative effect can result. Admittedly, the Constitutional Court can greatly encourage integration by securing legal peace; but this value is undermined, as is the legitimacy of the political system, when, as a result of pressures in the constitutional system, the Constitutional Court usurps parliamentary functions. The Basic Treaty case illustrated how this could happen.[36]

Notes

[1] Interview published in the official *Bulletin*, Federal Press and Information Office, 15 August 1974.

[2] Karl Jaspers, *The Future of Germany*, Chicago and London 1965.

[3] Kurt Sontheimer, *Antidemokratisches Denken in der Weimarer Republik*, Munich 1962. See particularly Chapter 3.

[4] This view is put by Richard Löwenthal, 'Vom kalten Krieg zur Ostpolitik' in *Die zweite Republik. 25 Jahre Bundesrepublik Deutschland − eine Bilanz*, Stuttgart 1974, p.693.

[5] Alexander und Margarete Mitscherlich, *Die Unfähigkeit zu trauern*, Munich 1967. See particularly Chapter 1.

[6] Cf. Peter Ludz, 'Social change in the FRG and the GDR', in: *Teaching Postwar Germany in America*, Institute of German Studies, Indiana University, 1972, p.74.

[7] Peter Ludz, *Deutschlands doppelte Zunkunft*, Munich 1974, pp.79 ff.

[8] Cf. Ghita Ionescu and Isabel de Madariaga, *Opposition*, London 1968, p.9.

[9] Ralf Dahrendorf, *Gesellschaft und Demokratie in Deutschland*, Munich 1965, pp.161−244.

[10] Ernst Fraenkel, 'Strukturdefekte der Demokratie und deren Überwindung' in Ernst Fraenkel und Kurt Sontheimer, *Zur Theorie der pluralistischen Demokratie*, Bundeszentrale für Politische Bildung, Bonn 1964, pp.8−16.

[11] The term stems from Otto Kirchheimer's article 'Germany: the vanishing opposition' in Robert A. Dahl (ed.), *Political Oppositions in Western Democracies*, London 1965, p.237.

[12] Robert Leicht, *Grundgesetz und politische Praxis*, Munich 1974, pp.78 ff.

[13] Ibid., p.80.

[14] Hans-Peter Schwarz, 'Wie wird es weitergehen? in Richard Löwenthal and Hans-Peter Schwarz, *Die Zweite Republik . . .*, p.947.

15   Ibid.

16   Ibid., p.948.

17   For a recent statement, see Kurt Sontheimer, *The Government and Politics of West Germany,* London 1972, p.70.

18   Dahrendorf, op. cit., pp.260–76.

19   From a translation of the Basic Law by the Linguistic Section of the West German Foreign Office, published in 1973 by the Federal Press and Information Office.

20   Author's italics.

21   *Entscheidungen des Bundesverfassungsgerichts* nos. 5, 85.

22   Judgement of the Federal Constitutional Court of 31 July 1973, quoted in Leicht, op. cit., p.93.

23   Leicht, op. cit., p.94. The analysis in the following pages closely follows that in Chapter 4 of Leicht's book, which is recommended as a lucid short account of the role of the constitution in West German politics.

24   Ibid.

25   *Neue juristische Wochenschrift,* 1973, p.1544; quoted in Leicht, op. cit., p.95.

26   Ibid.

27   Ibid., p.97.

28   Ibid., p.111.

29   Cf. Wilhelm Hennis, 'Verfassung und Verfassungswirklichkeit. Ein deutsches Problem' *Recht und Staat* Nos. 373–4, Tübingen 1974, p.21.

30   Ibid., p.7.

31   Hennis lists a large number of works (op. cit., p.6), the titles of which are variations on the *Verfassung* versus *Verfassungswirklichkeit* theme.

32   Quoted in Hennis, op. cit., p.22.

33   *Numerus clausus* denotes restricted entry to universities. Traditionally anybody with a school-leaving certificate *(Abitur)* has had the right to go to university.

34   Cf. Leicht, op. cit., p.138.

35   Ibid., p.139.

36   Ibid., p.120.

1 The Ostpolitik and Régime Stability in West Germany

W. E. PATERSON*

> As somebody once said, the Federal Republic ought to recognise itself — and precisely that is a part of the foreign policy that we are striving to develop at present.
>
> Willy Brandt, *Die Zeit,* 29 October 1971

In the last decade there has appeared a flood of articles and monographs analysing the motivations and implications of the *Ost-* and *Deutschlandpolitik* of successive West German governments. These analyses have generally been pitched at the level of the impact of these policies on international politics. Where the impact of the *Ostpolitik* on the domestic arena has been analysed it has generally been in relation to the ostensible objects of the policy — i.e., the states of Eastern Europe.[1] This chapter is basically concerned with the impact of these policies on the stability of the Federal Republic. It will be argued that the *Ostpolitik* implies — as the above quotation from Brandt indicates — the Federal Republic's acceptance of itself, and that it has thus contributed decisively to the stability of West Germany. In particular, it will be argued that the Federal Republic's commitment to the re-creation of a pan-German state has been abandoned as a matter of practical policy. In this situation, it will be further argued that West Germany is beginning to display characteristics normally associated with the nation-state.

The concept of 'nation', although difficult to define, is still essential for any discussion of political stability and the viability of régimes, whether we are considering Ulster, Belgium or, indeed, the United Kingdom. This is nowhere more true than in the case of Germany, where it has formed the central point of political controversy for nearly two centuries. Up to the close of the eighteenth century, Germany was split into many small states, and progress towards a centrally governed state seemed very improbable as the constituent states were able to meet any challenge by

* The author would like to thank the Editor of *International Affairs* for permission to use large sections of an earlier article on 'Foreign Policy and Stability in West Germany' (*International Affairs,* July 1973, pp.413−30).

relying on a moderate form of enlightened absolutism. Even at that time there was a German nation, but it was a *Kulturnation*. Evolution along these lines was interrupted by the external force of the French Revolution. While there was considerable initial enthusiasm for the revolution, this gave way under the aggressive expansion of the French to a much stronger sense of German national consciousness, which was reflected in a desire to give it political expression by transforming Germany into a *Staatsnation*. Nationalism in Germany thus preceded the achievement of political unity.

The realisation of the national ideal in Germany demanded the physical defeat of Austria — which explains why the German *Nationalstaat* was created in 1871 under the auspices of Prussia. The failure of the liberals in 1848, the tradition of German thought about the state, and the success of Prussia meant that the idea of the 'nation' was identified with the values of an *Obrigkeitstaat* (authoritarian state) — that it was, in the words of Alfred Grosser, not based on *'le peuple-volonté de Michelet: bien plutôt le peuple-ethnie, le peuple troupeau docile à ses chefs temporels ou spirituels'.*[2] The new nation-state represented an unsatisfactory solution to the problem of creating a unified German state, since it excluded the Germans of the Austro-Hungarian Empire together with the Swiss Germans. It represented too an uneasy fusion between the imperial idea and the national ideal, emphasising, as it did, pre-national values. The considerable autonomy enjoyed by the states meant that Germany did not conform to the model of the unified nation-state typical by this time of Western Europe. The sense of national identity that this frail creation enjoyed stemmed mainly from action in the field of external policy, where fervent efforts were made to compensate for Germany's position as a 'belated nation' (Plessner).

The Weimar Republic, the successor state to the Empire, was seriously weakened by the inability of large sections of the population to identify it with the nation. This was the result not so much of the loss of territory, since relatively little had been lost, as of the Republic's failure to incorporate the predominantly conservative and autocratic values that had been identified with the Empire.[3]

The ability of Adolf Hitler to identify himself with these values played, as is well known, an important role in his rise to power. With the *Anschluss* of 1938 he achieved an almost complete coincidence of *Staatsnation* and *Kulturnation,* of the nation conceived of as a political entity and as a cultural, ethnic and linguistic concept. It was the first time that this had occurred. While it became increasingly apparent after the outbreak of the war that Hitler's goals were much more dynamic and

24

dangerous than asserting the power of the German nation, the coincidence of *Staatsnation* and *Kulturnation* was still strong enough to ensure that the defeat of Germany would mean the defeat of the nation as a whole. Not the least important aspect of this defeat was the moral one. On 20 July 1944, certain conservative resisters tried to escape this dilemma, by attempting to assassinate Hitler in the name of the values associated by them with the nation; but their efforts were doomed to failure, since they would have meant associating the nation with defeat.

Thus the end of the Nazi period meant the breakdown of an already fragile historical continuity. In this atmosphere, the idea of a German *Staatsnation* was attacked both by supporters of European unity and by particularists, especially in such states as Bavaria. This feeling that Germany had gambled away the right to be unified lessened as wartime memories receded, although nationalism of an aggressive, exclusive kind continued to be regarded with revulsion.

The Federal Republic's search for stability

When the Federal Republic was set up in 1949, great care was taken to stress its provisional character. It was given a 'Basic Law', not a constitution as such, and the Basic Law was not adopted by a referendum, which would have lent it too much legitimacy. The new state possessed no national anthem, although it was given a flag. An attempt by the first President, Theodor Heuss, to introduce a new national anthem was a total failure. (The German composer Karlheinz Stockhausen produced an ironic postscript to this episode in his composition *Hymnen*, which was an amalgam of forty national anthems). The Federal Republic was not fully a state, but rather a temporary mechanism for holding in trust the legal rights pertaining to Germany as a whole, meaning Germany within its 1937 boundaries. Its citizens were expected to owe only instrumental loyalty to the West German state; deeper loyalties were to be reserved for a future reunified Germany. These loyalties were legitimised in three ways: by the fact that the anti-Communist nature of the state genuinely reflected the views of the majority of its citizens; by free elections, which provided the basis of the Federal Republic's claim to be the sole legitimate representative of the German people *(Alleinvertretungsanspruch)*; and by the implicit understanding that acceptance of the Federal Republic would result in a relaxation of Allied controls and in increasing German prosperity.

In the first few years of the Federal Republic, federal politics revolved around what was to replace it, the main lines of internal policy having been decided before the establishment of the Republic.[4] This might have been anticipated from the provisions of the Basic Law, especially Article 24.1, which provides for the transfer of sovereign rights to international authorities; Articles 23 and 146, which are ambiguous as to whether the territory referred to is the Federal Republic of Germany, or Germany within its borders of 1937; and, perhaps most obviously, from the commitment of reunification expressed in the Preamble to the Basic Law. Dr Adenauer, the first Federal Chancellor, would have liked to see West Germany absorbed into a larger, West European grouping, the forces of German nationalism merged in a macro-European nationalism centred on a commitment to Catholicism and anti-Communism.[5] The existence of a large number of refugees in the Federal Republic made an unequivocal espousal of this standpoint impossible, and Adenauer preserved a verbal commitment to German unity. However, the circumstances of post-war Europe forced him to reject the Central European orientation that alone would have made a policy of reunification possible. West Germany was an occupied country, and if any policy were to succeed, it had to acknowledge this fact. As the Western powers were opposed to reunification except on terms known to be unacceptable to the Russians, Adenauer had little choice but to follow his natural inclinations and opt for integration with the West. Adenauer's genius was to identify the recovery of West German sovereignty with the integration of Western Europe. Under him, Germany re-emerged as a major power at the same time as it became a partner in the EEC and NATO. The two processes were simultaneous and almost indistinguishable, enabling Adenauer to identify the emergence of West Germany as a political force with the pattern of co-operation being established in the Western world. Thus West Germany was awarded the formal attributes of statehood — internal and external sovereignty — as a result of joining NATO in 1955. By following this policy Adenauer was able to bring about a profound reconcilation with France and yet avoid the stark alternatives of the past, when Germany either dominated the European system or was discriminated against by other powers.

Adenauer's policy was opposed by the Social Democratic Party (SPD), the main opposition party, which continued to give first priority to the task of reuniting the German nation within its 1937 borders.[6] It was felt that this nationalist strain in SPD policy offered a chance of appealing to the huge number of refugees in West Germany, who might otherwise be attracted to a new totalitarian movement and prevent the SPD from being identified with a policy of fulfilment. At a higher level, it offered a chance of shifting the identification with the nation from its historic position on the Right, and thus of overcoming some of what the SPD could only regard as its pathological qualities. A nationalist policy would, it was hoped, give the party some hope of breaking out of the traditional minority camp. The danger that the party might be permanently confined to a minority position had been increased by the loss of former SPD strongholds in the East. This nationalism was in no danger of being outbid from the Right, since extreme nationalist groups were likely to be outlawed either by the Federal Consititutional Court or directly by the Allies. This assumption was proved correct in October 1952, when the SRP, a neo-Nazi party, was outlawed by the Federal Constitutional Court, and in 1953, when British security authorities broke up an attempted takeover of sections of the Free Democratic Party (FDP) by neo-Nazi elements under the leadership of Werner Naumann, Göbbels' former State Secretary. The nationalist opposition to Adenauer established by Kurt Schumacher was continued by his successor as party chairman, Erich Ollenhauer. But the party was wrong in its calculation that a stress on nationalism would bring in sufficient refugee votes to sway the balance of power in the Federal Republic. Enough refugees were attracted to the Christian Democratic Union (CDU) by the strength of its anti-Communism and by their share in the growing prosperity of the Federal Republic — which was made possible by the Equalisation of the Burden Laws of 1952 — to prevent any change in the balance of power.

The SPD nationalist opposition to European integration, which had been at its most intense when the question of European integration became identified with that of defence, softened after the two were separated by German entry into NATO in 1955, and as the prospects of German unity began to appear more remote. Other contributory factors were the return of the Saar to Germany, the interest in Euratom, and the positive experience of prominent Social Democrat leaders, such as Herbert Wehner, in the Common Assembly of the European Coal and Steel Community.

In October 1955, the SPD was able to join the Monnet Committee as a founding member, and thereafter its leaders became enthusiastic 'Europeans', their views coinciding with government policy over the whole field of European integration. In retrospect these years can be characterised as the 'Monnet years', when the West German citizen, happy in his role as *homo economicus,* gave less and less thought to the problems of his identity, and elections, in the words of Erich Kuby, became 'plebiscites for refrigerators'.[7]

This period beginning in 1955 was one of stability in the Federal

Republic. Various factors contributed to this stability, but one of the main ones was anti-Communism. It is difficult to overestimate its importance, for it was in effect the political cement that held West Germany together. All the major parties were in agreement here, and the SPD, though in favour of reunification, was just as anti-Communist as the CDU — indeed more so in some ways. Anti-Communism provided a way of integrating the refugees into the structure, as well as the economic prosperity of West Germany, for they were in the paradoxical position of being extremely anti-Communist while being in favour of reunification.

Closely connected to anti-Communism as a factor relating to stability was economic prosperity. This was extremely important and was conditional on European integration, though not in the way that people think about it in Britain, in the sense that the expansion of markets might lead to greater prosperity. The directly economic arguments are less important. With hindsight, one can see that it was only because West Germany accepted the constraints of an integration framework that other countries agreed to the production ceilings imposed on West German industry being lifted.

Anti-Communism and economic prosperity together helped to produce stability in West Germany. Indirectly, they also helped to remove potential instability, for it was a combination of these two factors that conditioned the SPD to move to the Right. However, this stability was of a very odd kind, being based on what Stephen Warnecke calls a political narcosis, or an absence of discussion.[8] Anti-Communism integrated people into the system in a negative way. Moreover, whilst one can say that economic prosperity was the mark of a more positive type of integration, the level of attachment to the system was of course very low, and bound to be so, since the system prevented people from identifying with the Federal Republic. The West German political élite would have been very worried if mass identification with West Germany had been much higher, since that would have been seen as being a reflection on the then primary goal, reunification. Obviously, anti-Communism meant that the range of political debate was narrowed and participation low, and the commitment to reunification implied a low degree of attachment to the political institutions of the Federal Republic. It was, then, a fragile stability and one that was subject to change; a collapse in West Germany's economic prosperity would naturally have threatened it most. This did not happen. The 1960s were, however, dominated by the collapse of the Adenauer solution of the German problem. It is this, together with the attendant decline of anti-Communism and the increasing unreality of reunification, that has really changed the situation.

28

The collapse of the Adenauer solution

The Adenauer solution to what was coming to be called the German *question* rather than the German *problem* was almost universally accepted by the late 1950s. Early in 1960, the SPD abandoned its last independent initiative, the *Deutschlandplan* of 1959. Yet, as so often happens once a solution is universally accepted, the first cracks in the foundation supporting it began to appear, and the 1960s were dominated by its collapse.

Adenauer's conception of West Germany involved, as we have seen, its participation in a supranational political grouping of West Europe states, and eventually in the creation of a United States of Europe. This view came under extreme pressure from the policies of Gaullist France, policies that Adenauer felt impelled to support because of his belief in the overriding necessity for a Franco-German *entente*. Ironically, General de Gaulle's assertion of the French nation can be considered as an important contributory factor in the formation of an embryonic West German nation. But the Franco-German Friendship Treaty of 1963 soon proved to be a dead letter, and Gaullist policy, culminating in the precipitation of the Community crisis of 1965 and the subsequent Luxembourg Agreements of January 1966, made any development towards a truly supranational West European union extraordinarily improbable. The prospects for such a union were further weakened by the accession of Willy Brandt to the Chancellorship in September 1969. Although Brandt played a major role in the Hague summit conference of that year and in the subsequent extension of the Community, most of his energies were taken up with the preparation of pan-European solutions, and he declared himself to be against a West European federal state.[9] The accession of the three new members to the Community in January 1973, has almost certainly weakened the already slim prospects for some form of genuine political union.

Progress at a societal level has been equally slow. We now have enough evidence to conclude that it has not been possible to create a viable European macro-nationalism. There has been no large-scale transference of political loyalties on the part of individual citizens, and it is difficult to avoid endorsing Karl Deutsch's conclusion that 'European integration has slowed down since the mid-Fifties and has reached a plateau since 1958.'[10] This point has been made very succinctly by Donald Puchala.[11] After a detailed examination of public opinion surveys, he concludes that, 'Whatever integration in Western Europe meant institutionally and otherwise between 1954 and 1962, it apparently did not mean the submergence of nationalities in a transnational population.'

Reunification becomes increasingly unreal

More threatening to the previously held conception of the Federal Republic has been the consolidation of the German Democratic Republic. The legitimacy of West Germany has always to some extent depended on the visible weakness of the GDR. The events of 1953 in Berlin helped to legitimise the Federal Republic in the eyes of its citizens, as can be seen very clearly from the fact that 17 June, unlike 20 July (the anniversary of the attempted assassination of Hitler in 1944), became a major national holiday in West Germany. This view of the GDR, based on the fundamentally anti-Communist nature of the origin of the Federal Republic, meant that German unity was looked upon as a result of the collapse of the GDR, not as a result of the growing together of the two Germanies. For this reason, West German policy, as enshrined in the Hallstein Doctrine of 1955, which labelled recognition of the GDR by a foreign power as an unfriendly act, was designed to weaken the East German régime. Paradoxically, however, the confession of weakness that the régime made in 1961, by building the Berlin Wall, has resulted in a consolidation of the GDR. Having deprived its population of the right to flee, the East German government embarked on a process of liberalisation in the economic field. With a population one-third of that of the Federal Republic, the GDR became Europe's fifth industrial power and the second trading nation in the Eastern bloc, contributing one-fifth of the Soviet Union's total import requirements. As far as one can judge, the GDR *Staatsbürger* has proved to be as much a *homo economicus* as his West German neighbour; and the progress of the economy and the manner in which the rewards of this progess have been distributed have strengthened his loyalty to the régime, resulting in the creation of a GDR consciousness.[12]

In one sense this was easier to accomplish in East Germany than in the Federal Republic. Although the East German leadership has co-operated even more closely with its allies than the Federal Republic has with its, and although the political system of the GDR was, in the sense that Rosenau uses the word, more 'penetrated',[13] integration at a societal level was never possible given the historical context of Eastern Europe. This allowed a great stress on national, particularly Prussian, values. This process has been accompanied by an abandonment of East Germany's earlier endorsement of the goal of German unity.

In April 1968, the GDR adopted a new constitution that emphasised its distinctness from West Germany and proclaimed it to be a 'Socialist state of the German people'. At the same time the Secretariat for All-German Affairs was renamed the Secretariat for East German Affairs. This trend has become more dominant in recent months, and, as part of the official policy of *Abgrenzung* (demarcation), the GDR has now been categorised as a 'nation' by leading East German functionaries. This policy is likely to become more marked as contacts between the peoples of the two states increase. In one of his last speeches, on 14 January 1971, Walter Ulbricht referred to the development of a socialist national culture in the GDR. Simultaneously, there has been a great increase in the international recognition accorded to East Germany. This process of consolidation was a serious challenge to Adenauer's policy, which had held out the hope that a strong and united Western Europe would eventually persuade the Soviet Union to hand over East Germany. In this connection, Melvin Croan advanced what he claimed to be an empirically derived theorem of intra-German politics: 'the impossibility of stabilising one part of the divided nation without seriously threatening to destabilise the other part'.[14]

Adenauer's policy was further weakened by the changed attitude of the United States. The new Kennedy Administration made it clear that it intended to press for a *détente* with the Soviet Union despite the continued division of Germany. It had been one of Adenauer's major diplomatic successes that he had obtained the Allies' assurance that any *détente* would be predicated on a solution of the German question. Now, it was no longer possible to identify complete loyalty to the West with support of German unity. This fact became even clearer during the Johnson and Nixon Administrations. President Johnson, for instance, failed to mention the problem of Germany in his important 'building bridges' speech of October 1966.

These developments had a significant effect on the population of West Germany. Public belief in, and concern with, reunification and the related question of the Oder-Neisse Line dropped sharply throughout the 1960s. Uwe Kitzinger claimed from his reading of survey data that, by 1969, reunification was considered the most important task of a West German government by only 6 per cent of the electorate.[15] Even more revealing are the figures cited by Josef Korbel. In 1956, the partition of Germany was considered 'intolerable' by 52 per cent; in 1962, by 61 per cent; and, in 1963, by 53 per cent. The proportion dropped to 38 per cent in 1965, and 22 per cent in 1966.[16] In 1955, 58 per cent of West Germans polled believed that the United States was in favour of reunification, but in 1969

31

only 37 per cent thought so.[17]

The waning of public commitment to the primacy of German reunification as a goal of state policy was complemented by a similar decline at the élite level. West German business interests, anxious to expand their markets in Eastern Europe and fearful of the social and political effects of reunification have been the most ready of the various élite groups to contemplate an end to its primacy. The trade unions, which earlier had been enthusiastic about the prospect of transforming the Federal Republic through the incorporation of the more Socialist elements of the GDR, became less enthusiastic as their commitment to Socialism waned, and they have followed the Social Democrat line on foreign policy very closely.[18] One of the lasting weaknesses of any policy based on reunification is that no group in West Germany has an obvious economic interest in it; even in 1959 the majority of West Germans were not prepared to make an economic sacrifice for German unity.[19]

In post-war Germany, especially in the Federal Republic, the churches have played an important role in politics. While the Roman Catholic Church has been an important source of support for policies of West European integration, the Protestant Church has been strongly identified with the cause of German unity. The importance of the Protestant 'Memorandum on the situation of the refugees and the relationship of the German people to their Eastern neighbours' (published in October 1965), which accepted that the Poles also had a *Recht auf Heimat,* was thus, in the words of Karl Kaiser, impossible to overemphasise.[20] This report marked a real change in the attitude of the German Evangelical Church, and reunification could no longer be counted as one of its primary political demands. This change culminated, in May 1970, in the election of Ludwig Raiser, the main author of the Memorandum, to the Presidency of the synod of the Evangelical Church.

The strongest support for a policy based on German reunification came from sections of the army and the diplomatic service. But the views of the army have been fairly unimportant, due to its low status and low access to the decision-making process. The views of most members of the diplomatic service have changed in response to the changing domestic climate and international situation, and those who continue to cling to the primacy of German reunification have been forced to resort to leaks to the Springer Press, since their official position prevents them from saying anything openly. This general lessening of interest has been mirrored in the spectacular decline in the prestige and intellectual coherence of *Kuratorium Unteilbares Deutschland,* the most important pressure group concerned with the propagation of German reunification.

This process has been accompanied by a drastic decline in the bargaining position of the refugees. A refugee party, the *Block der Heimatvertriebenen und Entrechteten,* founded in January 1950, won twenty-seven seats in the 1953 election. The desertion to the CDU of its two most prominent representatives, Kraft and Oberländer, proved fatal, and it was not represented in the third Bundestag. Another vehicle for the views of refugees, the Gesamtdeutsche Partei: (GDP), polled only about 2·8 per cent of the votes in 1961. The refugees' hopes of influencing the two major parties have also dwindled with the death of their major spokesmen, H.C. Seebohm in the CDU, and Wenzel Jaksch in the SPD. Seebohm, despite his undoubted expertise as Transport Minister (he had been a minister for sixteen years), was excluded from office on the formation of the new government in 1965, his views having become an embarrassment to any policy of *détente.* Wenzel Jaksch, president of the refugees association, was killed in a traffic accident in November 1966. More important, there was a growing discrepancy between the views of the aging functionaries of the refugee movements, and those of their sons and daughters and the West German population at large. [21] Although they fought a vigorous rearguard action, they suffered continual reversals during the 1960s, culminating in the debacle of the 1969 election. In October 1969, the Ministry for Refugees was abolished. A great deal of attention was focused on Herbert Hupka, the Silesian refugee leader and the last prominent spokesman for the refugees' cause within the SPD, when he deserted to the Christian Democrats in the spring of 1972, and there was some speculation about the revival of refugee influence. In fact, the refugee organisations played no discernible role in the elections of November 1972.

Finally, the Adenauer solution suffered from the changing attitudes of the political parties, particularly the FDP and SPD. Despite its smallness, the Free Democratic Party has played a crucial role, due to the balance of forces in the Federal Republic. Initially it acted as a valuable safety valve in the Adenauer consensus, by laying more stress on *Ostpolitik* while generally, though not universally, accepting the steps taken by the Chancellor in furthering West European integration. Throughout the 1960s, the FDP, influenced by the reformers Schollwer, Rubin and Scheel, and by the desertion of many of its conservative voters, first to the CDU and then also to the National Democratic Party (NPD), softened its anti-Communism more quickly than the two major parties. What ex-Chancellor Kiesinger called the *Anerkennungspartei* ('recognition party') has been more strongly represented in the FDP than in the two major parties. [22] However, the change that took place in the position of the SPD was even more important. Under the pressure of world events, particularly in Berlin, the SPD gradually ceased to give primacy to the goal of reunification, and instead gave greater emphasis to a West German contribution to *détente* and to the improvement of living conditions in the GDR. These interrelated developments have found expression in the *Ostpolitik* of successive West German governments.

The development of an Ostpolitik

The beginnings of an *Ostpolitik* were made under the CDU Foreign Minister Gerhard Schröder, who took up contacts, particularly at a trade level, with East European states. This policy had two main aims: first, to prevent the Federal Republic from being diplomatically isolated from the West, particularly from the United States; and, secondly, to isolate the GDR from its neighbours. No great progress was made though, since the continued operation of the Hallstein Doctrine prevented the establishment of diplomatic relations with states that also recognised East Germany. The establishment of the Grand Coalition in 1966, with Brandt succeeding to the post of Foreign Minister, led to a slightly faster rate of change. The Hallstein Doctrine was ignored in practice and relations were re-established with Yugoslavia and Romania. However, the possibility of any great change was circumscribed by the need for the coalition partners to agree, which became more difficult as the CDU recovered confidence.

The early days of the Brandt government in 1969 were marked by some fairly dramatic pronouncements, particularly in relation to East Germany. Perhaps the most famous of these was Brandt's reference to 'two states of one German nation', which, while stopping short of full international recognition of the GDR, also by implication ruled out, for the foreseeable future, the reunification option. Brandt's government declaration of 1969 was the first not to use the term 'reunification'. This meant that Brandt recognised that the pursuit of a policy based on the primacy of reunification had resulted in the atrophying of contacts between East and West Germany by encouraging the government of the GDR to maintain its defensive posture. Explicit acceptance of the fact that reunification was not practical policy would, it was hoped, enable the East German government to feel free enough to liberalise contacts between the two states and thus strengthen the sense of *Zusammengehörigkeitsgefühl* (feeling of belonging together). Historically, this feeling has not, as Brandt constantly emphasised, depended on living within the same frontiers. In other words, the new government, in the hope of preserving the German nation as a *Kulturnation*, refrained from stressing the pursuit of a German *Staatsnation*. Meetings were held between Brandt and Stoph, the Prime Minister of the GDR, at Erfurt and Kassel, but the East German leadership proved very unresponsive. Closer contacts between the two German states and their populations were still regarded in East Berlin as a real danger, a view reinforced by the pro-Brandt demonstrations at Erfurt and by riots in the Polish Baltic towns.

The Brandt government concluded treaties with the Soviet Union and with Poland in August and December of 1970. A similar agreement was concluded with Czechoslovakia in December 1973. The agreements with the Soviet Union and Poland offer these countries considerable economic benefits, but their main importance lies in the recognition of the territorial *status quo* in Europe (Article 1 of the Warsaw Treaty, Article 3 of the Moscow Treaty). The force of this is scarcely affected by the letter sent by the West German Foreign Minister, Walter Scheel, to the Soviet Foreign Minister on 12 August 1970. This letter, which was sent on the same day as the Moscow Treaty was signed, was written at a time when the government had been under heavy pressure as a result of 'leaks' to the Springer Press. The smallness of the government's majority meant that this gesture had to be made if the treaties were to have any hope of being ratified. It was also necessary to square them with the Basic Law. At Scheel's instigation, the Federal government insisted that a precondition for the ratification of these agreements must be a satisfactory settlement on Berlin. Its main demands were fulfilled in September 1971, with the conclusion of the Four-Power Agreement on Berlin.

However, by far the most important agreement for this discussion is the Basic Treaty regulating relations with East Germany. The contents of this treaty became known a fortnight before the Federal elections on 19 November 1972, and the treaty itself was signed on 22 December. In effect, it amounts to recognition of the GDR. Article 3 talks of the inviolability of the existing border and commits both states to unqualified respect for each other's territorial integrity. Article 6 recognises un-conditionally the internal and external sovereignty of both states. After the ratification of the treaty, both German states became members of the UN.

The importance of these developments has often been misconstrued, due to paying too much attention to their effects on East Germany. More important than this, though less dramatic in the short run, will be the effects on the Federal Republic. Recognition of the GDR has meant that it is possible for the first time fully to recognise the Federal Republic. It has also made it possible to begin developing a specifically West German nationhood, thus greatly increasing the chances of political stability in West Germany.

The 'nation', in the *Staatsnation* sense, can be described as the largest group of people who feel that they share a common identity, and who express (or wish to express) through political institutions their attachment to a defined spatial area. A member of such a nation feels a sense of 'otherness' towards citizens of all other states. This would, for instance, cover the Swiss case. In the following section, we shall discuss four main aspects of the emergence of a West German 'nation': the internal integration of the Federal Republic; the modalities of stability in West Germany; the growing sense of identity felt by citizens of the Federal Republic, and their estrangement from East Germany; and the impact of international politics.

There has been a marked tendency towards integration within West Germany. In addition to the integration of refugees, which has already been noted, there has been growing criticism of the notion of Federalism. Influential publicists like Theo Sommer have repeatedly pointed out the difficulties that the dual control of finances (a feature of the West German version federalism) pose for the preservation of an active defence and, thus, for foreign policy. [23] The more mobile that West German society becomes, the more federalism is perceived as a major hindrance to the solution of very important problems, such as education, law and order, and the environment.

This attack on federalism is implicitly an attack on the particularist loyalties that were so prominent at the time of the creation of the Federal Republic. There is no longer, as there was in 1949, a Bavarian question. Indeed, the balance of the religious denominations inside the Federal Republic means that Bavaria can be a part of the West German political community in a way that it could never be part of the Wilhelmine Empire.

In the first part of this chapter it was shown that, during the 1950s, a denial of the Federal Republic's permanence was a condition of its stability. In the 1960s the ground rules changed, and stability seems to have lain in asserting the permanence of the Federal Republic. The episode of the NPD helped to create an awareness of the fragility of a state based solely on a consensus grouped around economic prosperity and anti-Communism; and there have been signs, within the West German élite, of a broader appreciation of the need to overcome this deficiency in West German political culture by developing a feeling of identification with the West German state. This view, first articulated by the late Professor Besson, has been echoed by politicians like the present Chancellor, Helmut Schmidt, who has written of the need to identify 'with the *Gemeinschaft* [community] that exists within the state and nation'.[24]

The first SPD/FDP government was committed to a policy of internal reform as well as external *détente*. This policy, which was stymied by the operation of the federal system, was intended to help deepen loyalties to the West German state. The German federal system tends to block any far-reaching internal changes, due to the prominent role it accords to represenatives of the *Länder* in the law-making process. Since no one party has dominated government at both the Federal level and the *Land* level, there is great pressure for the preservation of the *status quo*. Even prominent Christian Democrat politicians like Olaf von Wrangel are calling for a consolidation of the Federal Republic. This contrasts strongly with the mid-1960s, when conservatives like Eugen Gerstenmaier and Gerhard Schröder tried to revive traditional pan-German national feelings. [25] On the societal level, an important piece of evidence is provided by Lutz Niethammer: more West Germans (41 per cent as against 38 per cent) now understand the expression 'our national interests' to mean those of the Federal Republic than see it as meaning the interests of the two German states. [26] At the level of personal observation, the undertone of irony and lack of pride that many observers found in the West Germans' description of themselves as *Bundesrepublikaner* has largely disappeared.

The greatest contribution to the development of deeper feelings of identification with the Federal Republic has been made, as the quotation from Brandt at the beginning of this chapter suggests, in the field of *Ost-* and *Deutschlandpolitik*. In recognising the sovereignty, permanence and separateness of the GDR, the West German government has at last accepted the permanent legitimacy of its own régime. The extent to which this self-acceptance has increased the stability and viability of the régime is shown by some features of the elections of November 1972.[27]

These elections are generally agreed to have been the most polarised in the history of the Federal Republic. Not only was party competition exceptionally fierce, but, in addition, the principal interest groups in West German society aligned themselves clearly with one or other of the main parties. Even more exceptionally, the degree of public involvement and debate was unprecedentedly high. Membership of the main political parties increased steadily throughout 1972; so did the liveliness of their debates. For the first time, many West German citizens were prepared to talk publicly about their political views, to advertise them in newspapers, and even to join 'voters' initiatives'. These 'voters' initiatives', although they supported one particular party, were not tied organisationally to the main parties and adopted an attitude of what can best be described as 'critical support' towards them. Finally, it is significant that the election was won by a coalition that was perceived by the voters (all opinion polls agree on this) as likely to be less efficient than the opposition at managing the economy.

Taken together, these features indicate that large numbers of people are now taking the permanency of the system seriously enough for them to take an active part in politics, and that there is a sufficient underlying consensus for the system to tolerate a high level of polarisation. That this consensus was provided by *Ostpolitik* can readily be demonstrated. *Ostpolitik* was the only issue on which the government enjoyed a clear advantage over the opposition (73 per cent to 9 per cent), and a survey undertaken by Marplan on 20 November 1972, indicated that 79 per cent of those polled thought that the Basic Treaty had been the most important single event to benefit the coalition. Moreover, the fact that the coalition could win despite being perceived by the voters to be less efficient at managing the economy is another indication that a régime whose stability has been held to be overdependent on economic success is broadening the basis of its support and the public developing affective ties to the political system.

Some have contended that this increased identification brought about by *Ostpolitik* was, in contrast to the argument developed above, dangerous to the stability of the Federal Republic. First of all, there was the danger of provoking the refugees. We have already seen that this was an unreal danger, since the refugees had already been integrated. Public opinion surveys throughout the 1960s indicated that the government had greater freedom of manoeuvre on such matters as recognition of East Germany than it believed it had. Secondly, it could be held that it was particularly dangerous to fight an election on an issue that involved defining such basic concepts as the 'state' and the 'nation'. These matters have traditionally caused a tremendous amount of trouble in Germany, as they have in Britain (though this did not become clear to the British, who had managed to forget about the Irish issue for such a long time, until relatively recently). In the present case, the risk would appear to have been unreal, as there was, at that time, a fairly general consensus of the people at large. There was a very sharp contrast between the violence of the parliamentary talk about *Ostpolitik* and the complete absence of violence on the streets. In fact, the underlying consensus on the issue proved a very effective political resource for the SPD in helping it to win that election, though it should be said that the political effectiveness of the resource has since been reduced, the concrete results of *Ostpolitik* having been disappointing. [28] In addition, the major decisions on *Ostpolitik* have a 'once and for all' character. In the 1950s, Adenauer identified a consensus on European integration, and was able to continue winning with this because European integration was a continually developing programme. With *Ostpolitik,* however, there is no longer any electoral advantage to be gained now that the big decisions have been taken and the big treaties, for which the necessary consensus was obtained, concluded.

Paradoxically, *Ostpolitik* may have done a great deal to destabilise the SPD. The post-war SPD has, given its past history, been curiously free from factional splits. Unity on the main issues stemmed largely from anti-Communism, which provided a social cement to hold the party together and keep the Left quiet. The type of *Ostpolitik* that the SPD has advanced is obviously conditional on a decline in anti-Communism, and interacts with that decline; it relies on perceptions about the GDR that are very different from those of the 1950s. One result of the decline in anti-Communism has been a widening of the range of political discussion. This, however, leads to a challenge to the SPD leadership, due to the revival of the Left wing and the revival of Marxist-type language, both of which are very unpopular electorally. In other words, some of the long-term results of *Ostpolitik* may prove to be destabilising to the SPD, though they are unlikely to be destabilising to the West Germany polity as a whole. The pressure from the Left in the SPD is seen by many people (not least the party leadership) to be extraordinarily vexatious, particularly as the party is by no means intimately connected with the GDR. If, however, conditions were to loosen up and the Left wing were seen to be intimately involved with developments there, then that could be seriously destabilising, due to the danger of overreaction from the Right. This would not seem to be the case, though there are some elements of this situation in, for instance, the proposals for laws to make it very difficult for radicals to find a place in the Civil Service. This can be seen as the West German *Abgrenzung.* On balance, however, it can be said that the *Ostpolitik*, inasmuch as it leads to identification, has heightened participation and is a positive contribution to stability. The dangers that it presents are mainly dangers to the SPD's electoral chances.

Although the Federal government is reluctant to accord full international recognition to the GDR, since this would imply that East Germany is 'abroad', there is little doubt that it is coming to seem more and more foreign to the citizens of the Federal Republic. This trend was apparent as early as 1963, when a group of journalists from *Die Zeit* entitled their report on a visit to the GDR 'Journey in a foreign land'.

Lutz Niethammer cites the 1967 public opinion survey that claimed that 79 per cent of the respondents felt that the two states were becoming more dissimilar. He also claims, from a reading of several empirical surveys, that the tendency to regard the GDR as 'foreign' is much more pronounced among younger age groups. [29] While this trend is obviously a product of the lack of contact between the two societies in past years, it is very doubtful if the new opportunities for travel to East Germany resulting from the conclusion of the Basic Treaty will reverse it, since young people in the two states have had completely different social upbringings. If the increased contact were to lead to a real *Zusammengehörigkeitsgefühl* on the part of East German citizens (especially younger citizens), it is likely that contact would again be made much more difficult. Even the present level of contact has led the East German leadership to pursue a policy of *Abgrenzung*.

However, the strongest reason for positing the existence of a West German nation lies in the field of foreign policy. First, and most obviously, the permanence of present boundaries has been accepted. Secondly, there is the new mood of self-assertion in foreign policy, and this in a country where identity has often been created by international action. 'To rejuvenate the country by way of foreign policy is an idea ever alive in the German tradition' (Besson). This mood of self-assertion, exemplified by Brandt's visit to Yalta in September 1971 and the conclusion of the Basic Treaty, is shown even more clearly by the monetary policies that West Germany has adopted in relation to the EEC since Helmut Schmidt's accession to the Chancellorship. It has been made possible by the decay of West Germany's dependence on the Western Allies, the result of a desire for support on Berlin and German reunification. In other words, a downgrading of the Federal government's role as spokesman for all German interests permits an upgrading of the specific interests of the Federal Republic. The presence of two Germanies in the United Nations has encouraged the feeling of separate identity. Even the measure of international recognition enjoyed by the GDR before the conclusion of the Basic Treaty had influenced the Federal government to delimit and, thus, emphasise the separate identity of the Federal Republic. [30]

Conclusion

It has been the argument of this chapter that the maintenance of the present régime in West Germany, on which so many hopes for stability in

Western Europe rest, has involved the creation of loyalties to the West German state that go beyond mere pragmatism and are more like the sort of loyalties we normally associate with the concept of 'nation'.

One is only too conscious of how fragile this process of creating a West German nation is, subject as it is to changes in the international constellation. It is also, of course, implicitly against the Basic Law, a factor of considerable importance in a *Rechtsstaat* (constitutional state) like the Federal Republic. This is one of the factors that have led to the characteristic ambiguity in the Federal government's policy on this matter.[31]

One is also aware of the elusiveness of the identity that has been described above, and of the fact that the evidence used to support the present thesis rests on a very short time-span. To treat West Germany as a new state and then look at it purely from the viewpoint of 'nation' building would be, despite the obvious parallels between the situation of West Germany in 1949 and that of a colonial state, to oversimplify, given the diverse impact of German history. Yet it would be difficult to deny that some aspects of this West German nationhood do now exist. Nationhood, like any form of loyalty, is, as Dankwart Rustow reminds us, a matter of degree: 'a given people at a given time may be more or less a nation, while none approximates the ideal type'.[32]

In the opening section of this chapter, we saw how much the content of the nation has altered historically. The further deepening of the attachment of West Germans to the Federal Republic will present much greater problems than did the similar process that took place in post-war Austria. Austria had a number of advantages: its core area was a recognisable historical entity; it had tried before (after the First World War); and, perhaps most important of all, retained its capital, Vienna. [33] Yet, given the lack of convincing alternative sources of allegiance, the prospects for West German nationhood seem fairly bright. The events of the last twenty-five years have shown to the West Germans, as the Second World War demonstrated to the Austrians, that other states will do nothing to bring about a pan-German state. Squaring the circle by means of European unity now looks equally unpromising. In the case of West Germany and in the circumstances outlined above, it now seems possible to talk in terms of an Austrian-type 'nation' — that is, a *Staatsnation,* but not a *Kulturnation.*

Notes

[1] Karl Kaiser's *German Foreign Policy in Transition* London 1968;

41

reviewed in *International Affairs,* October 1969, p.730) is the most notable exception to this rule.

[2] See A. Grosser, 'Spécificités du nationalisme allemand' in *La Revue d'Allemagne,* 1969, pp.421–35 (particularly p.423).

[3] K. Sontheimer, 'Der antiliberale Staatsgedanke in der Weimarer Republik' in *Politische Vierteljahresschrift,* 1962, pp.25–42.

[4] See especially F.R. Allemann, 'Bonns verschränkte Fronten: Parteiensystem und internationale Politik' in *Der Monat* vol. 35, no. 209, February 1966.

[5] See Adenauer's *Erinnerungen,* 4 vols, Frankfurt and Hamburg 1965–68; K.D. Erdmann, *Adenauer in der Rheinlandpolitik nach dem ersten Weltkrieg,* Stuttgart 1966; and A. Baring, *Aussenpolitik in Adenauers Kanzlerdemokratie,* Munich 1969.

[6] For a detailed study of the development of SPD attitudes, see W.E. Paterson, *The SPD and European Integration*, D.C. Heath, 1974.

[7] For Monnet's views on Germany see J.B. Duroselle, 'General de Gaulle's Europe and Jean Monnet's Europe' in *The World Today,* January 1966.

[8] S. Warnecke, 'The future of Rightist extremism in West Germany' in *Comparative Politics,* July 1970, pp.629–82 (particularly pp.649–50).

[9] For the clearest statement of Brandt's views on this topic see G. Ziebura, *Die deutschfranzösichen Beziehungen seit 1945: Mythen und Realitäten,* Pfullingen 1970, pp.188–9. Helmut Schmidt has often expressed similar reservations about too far-reaching an integration.

[10] K. Deutsch, 'Integration and arms control in the European political environment' in *American Political Science Review,* 1966, p.355.

[11] D. Puchala, 'National distinctiveness and transnationality in West European public opinion 1954-62' in *Integration* no. 3, 1970, pp.278–9. See also the table in M. Koch, *Die Deutschen und ihr Staat,* Hamburg 1972, p.76, showing that almost two-thirds of the West German respondents (58 per cent, as against 43 per cent for France) did not expect their government to be superseded at some point in the future by a united Europe.

[12] See especially E. Schulz, 'Die DDR als Gegenspieler der Bonner Ostpolitik' in *Europa-Archiv* no. 8, 1971, pp.283–92.

[13] J. Rosenau, in B. Farrell (ed.), *Approaches to Comparative and International Politics* Illinois, 1966, p. 65.

[14] M. Croan, 'Bonn and Pankow – intra-German politics' in *Survey,* April 1968, p.78. Later in this chapter it is argued that the reverse has been true in the long run.

[15] *The Times,* 30 September 1969.

[16] Cited J. Korbel, *Detente in Europe*, Princeton, N. J. 1972, p.184. Reviewed in *International Affairs*, April 1973, p.247.

[17] Ibid., p.186.

[18] W. Hanrieder, *The Stable Crisis, Two Decades of German Foreign Policy*, New York and London 1970, p.139.

[19] E. P. Neumann, 'Wiedervereinigung und öffentliche Meinung' in *Die politische Meinung* vol. 9, 1964, pp.9–31.

[20] Karl Kaiser, *German Foreign Policy in Transition*, London 1971, p.38.

[21] For example, 62 per cent of refugees under the age of fifty supported the Warsaw Treaty, *(WDR Survey*, March 1971). For more data supporting this hypothesis, see Korbel, op. cit., p.158. See also G. Schweigler, *Nationalbewusstsein in der BRD und der DDR*, Düsseldorf 1973, Table 24, p.115, which indicates that the percentage of refugees not prepared to return to their former homeland had risen from 20 per cent in 1953 to 74 per cent in 1970.

[22] There is no acceptable account available in English of the FDP's transformation from a 'national party' to its present position. However, there are now several accounts in German: H. J. Thiele, *Die Deutschlandpolitik der FDP*, MA thesis, Bonn 1968; Kurt Körper, *FDP – Bilanz der Jahre 1960–66*, Cologne 1968; Rolf Zundel, *Die Erben des Liberalismus*, Freudenstadt 1971.

[23] Theo Sommer, 'Selbstmord des Föderalismus' in *Die Zeit*, February 1969.

[24] W. Besson, 'The Federal Republic's national interest' in *Aussenpolitik*, English edition no. 2, 1970, pp.123–35. Ralf Dahrendorf, in his seminal *Society and Democracy in Germany* (London 1968), implicitly endorsed this position in his plea for the Federal Republic to turn inward and abandon the primacy of foreign policy. F. R. Allemann, in the article cited in note 4, explains why this *Wendung nach innen* (turning inward) did not come in the early 1960s, when the replacement of Adenauer by Erhard and the SPD's talk of *Gemeinschaftsaufgaben* (communal tasks) made it look a likely prospect. See also Helmut Schmidt, 'Bisher nur eine Schönwetterdemokratie' in *Frankfurter Allgemeine Zeitung*, 5 August 1969, p.10.

[25] Eugen Gerstenmaier, *Neuer Nationalismus? von der Wandlung der Deutschen*, Stuttgart 1964; and Gerhard Schröder, *Wir brauchen eine heile Welt*, Düsseldorf 1963.

[26] L. Niethammer, 'Traditionen und Perspektiven der Nationalstaatlichkeit für die BRD' in *Aussenpolitische Perspektiven des Westdeutschen Staates*, vol. 2, Munich and Vienna 1972, p.54.

[27] For more detail, see R.E.M. Irving and W. E. Paterson, 'The West German parliamentary election of November 1972' in *Parliamentary Affairs,* Spring 1973, pp.218–39.

[28] See *Der Spiegel,* 15 April 1974. This is a report on a public opinion survey indicating considerable public disappointment with the concrete results of *Ostpolitik.* It should be emphasised that this disappointment does not mean that opinion is in favour of a reversal of the treaties, only that concrete results are not expected.

[29] Niethammer, *passim.*

[30] For example, *Die Welt,* (17 January 1972) refers to a request from the Ministry of Inner German Affairs to the Ministry of Economics and Finance that, to avoid confusion, the word 'Germany' be deleted and replaced by 'Federal Republic' in a trade agreement with Luxembourg. This policy appears to have emanated from the Chancellor's Office.

[31] Egon Bahr, for instance, has consistently maintained that he continues to see *Ostpolitik* in terms of eventual German reunification. The ambiguity in the policy of successive West German governments prompted Peter Bender to remark that 'the only way to introduce a new policy in the Federal Republic is to guarantee that it is merely a continuation of an old one'.

[32] Dankwart Rustow's article on 'Nation' in *The International Encyclopaedia of Social Science,* New York 1968.

[33] On Austria, see W. Bluhm, *Building an Austrian Nation: the Political Integration of a Western State,* New Haven, Conn., 1973.

2   The Ostpolitik and the Opposition in West Germany

Geoffrey PRIDHAM

The following comment of Ralf Dahrendorf's on foreign policy as the battleground for fundamentalist conflict between rival parties in West Germany is relevant to the question of the CDU/CSU opposition's attitude towards *Ostpolitik:*

> Dissension on issues of national importance involves a contest of absolute demands. There is no room for compromise between those who recognise the Oder-Neisse Line and those who want to remove it at any price. No change is possible in which the intensified discussion about the attitude of the Federal Republic towards the GDR may show itself to be more productive. Each side basically demands the unconditional conversion of his opponent. Differences in matters of national importance create an almost breathtaking, even deadly, climate in domestic politics.[1]

This statement is applicable to the opposition's attitude to Brandt's *Ostpolitik* for two reasons. The first is that fundamentalist opposition reaches its climax in the debate over external policy, and the second that this polarisation spills over into the arena of domestic politics, which in turn affects the legitimacy of the political system.

There are a number of striking parallels to the CDU/CSU's attitude, notably the way that the SPD opposition behaved towards Adenauer's *Westpolitik* in the 1950s. One sees in the CDU's behaviour after its loss of power, a sense of disappointment recalling the SPD's disappointment after not having gained power in 1949, against the expectations of many. Comparisons may also be drawn with the opposition of the British Labour Party to the Common Market. In the cases of the CDU and the Labour Party, a combination of three similar factors can be observed: first, normal opposition politics, heightened by the shock resulting from the loss of power (felt by the Labour Party in 1970); secondly, a principled objection to the policy in question at all levels of the party structure; and, thirdly, the influence on the party's attitude to the policy concerned, of tensions arising from the party's internal situation. In both cases a loss of credibility resulted from the party's stand on the particular issue. One major difference, however, is the fact that the CDU/CSU's attitude pushed it in a direction contrary to the general tendency of public opinion in West Germany, whereas the Labour Party's attitude to the Common Market has appeared to be more in accordance with public opinion in Britain. An even more important reason for the CDU's loss of credibility in opposition derives from the consensus-oriented nature of the West German electorate, which regards any outbreak of intense party conflict as offensive. This applies particularly in the present case, for the conflict followed the surface harmony of the Grand Coalition period.

One should at this point refer to the nature of opposition in Western Germany. This is influenced by certain characteristics of the party system there. While there has been, over the last decade or more, a growing uniformity of the party system — certainly at the Federal level, but also at the *Land* level — one still detects a considerable rigidity. This shows itself in the unreadiness of the major parties to change from government to opposition and *vice versa*. The first change of principal governing party occurred in 1969, when the Left–Liberal coalition of the SPD and FDP came to power; this event was accompanied by a number of statements emphasising how deeply the experience was felt. Brandt, in his government declaration of October 1969, claimed that the formation of the Left–Liberal coalition was the 'beginning of democracy' — not literally, in terms of the nature of the actual institutions of government, but rather in terms of the emphasis placed on democratic values. Even more provocative remarks issued from the opposition. A few months after Brandt became Chancellor, Franz-Josef Strauss, the CSU chairman, said that the *Machtwechsel* (change of power) was 'not a simple change of government according to the rules of parliamentary democracy, for it aims at introducing a fundamental and long-term reorientation in German politics both internally and externally'.[2]

This tendency to indulge in normative mudslinging was evident on various occasions during the sixth Bundestag (for instance, in the exchanges during the speech by the Minister of Finance in September 1970[3]), but it also reappeared after the 1972 election, which confirmed the *Machtwechsel* of 1969. Brandt's claim to represent the *die neue Mitte,* the new centre of West German politics, was hotly disputed by various opposition leaders. Karl Carstens, the new chairman of the CDU/CSU *Fraktion* (Parliamentary party), said, in a speech made early in 1974, that the CDU/CSU was the only really democratic party in Western Germany. By this he principally meant that the CDU was the upholder of the values of the social market economy, but he also had the *Ostpolitik* in mind, for his remark was coupled with a warning about the dangers accruing from

46

neutralist tendencies in foreign policy. The experience of the sixth Bundestag, with the reappearance of polarisation, has forced a modification of the Kirchheimer thesis of the 'vanishing opposition' in Western Germany. This claimed that the great controversy of the 1950s, specifically over foreign policy, had been replaced by a degree of consensus which rendered the survival of vigorous oppositional politics doubtful.[4]

The behaviour of the CDU/CSU opposition since 1969 shows that it has found it difficult to accept one primary characteristic of 'loyal' opposition. This was identified by Dr Bruno Heck, until 1971 the General Secretary of the CDU, in a significant speech he made at the Mainz Congress of the CDU in November 1969, when he said that it is normal for an opposition party to 'adjust in the long term to the governing parties over decisive questions'. Basically, the CDU did not really come round to accepting this; certainly not by the time of the 1972 election. There were, however, elements within the party that were at least tempted by the possibility of co-operation with the SPD/FDP coalition. Here one remembers the picture taken of Brandt and Barzel (the CDU leader) talking over glasses of beer in the Bundestag restaurant in May 1972, when the two sides were trying to work out an agreed formula on the general aims of foreign policy. A revealing remark was made by Dr Barzel in an interview he gave *Die Zeit* in December 1971, on the eve of his visit to Moscow. He commented that 'there is now an invitation to the leader of the opposition from the Soviet government', and that 'basically, our whole debate revolves around the consequences of an *Ostpolitik* that we have not created, and that the Federal government has undertaken alone against our good counsel.'[5] A governing party has the right to initiate policies, yet the implication here was that Brandt had acted against the wishes of the opposition and that this was a bad thing.

Essentially, the CDU/CSU opposition was grappling with two problems. First it had to adapt to the new and unwelcome role of opposition in a country with a political culture that is in many respects quite markedly executive-oriented, depriving political opposition to some extent of a certain legitimacy that it possesses in such countries as Britain. Secondly, the opposition was faced with the question of political norms, for, while it obviously had to continue working within the political system, it was, at the same time, becoming more and more concerned by what it saw as a challenge to the values upholding that system. The government had lessened its anti-Communism, which increased fundamentalist fears among the Christian Democrats. These problems had to be met at a time when the CDU was thrown back on its own resources after its loss of office and had to search for a new identity. The party's tergiversations and expressions of fundamentalist dislike were often a reflection of its own sense of insecurity, and accordingly the CDU/CSU's attitude in the *Ostpolitik* debate was partly a consequence of its difficulty in adapting to the unaccustomed role of opposition.

The problem of the opposition and the *Ostpolitik* will be discussed in two parts: first, the attitudes of the CDU/CSU to this particular government policy, and the reasons for them; and, secondly, the effect of the Ostpolitik debate on the party itself.

The public's overall impression of the CDU/CSU's position on the *Ostpolitik* was basically a negative one. This was so despite the fact that Barzel attempted to qualify the party's attitude by saying that it genuinely found itself unable to accept the policy. The public impression was justified in so far as the balance of opinion within the party was decisively tilted towards the negative side, though it is true that views held on controversial issues can appear simplified in their presentation to the public. In fact, attitudes within the party did vary to a significant degree. The party showed a peculiar lack of solidarity over the *Ostpolitik*, reminiscent of the divisions that the party experienced over *Westpolitik* in the mid 1960s, when Erhard was Chancellor. This time there was a similar conflict of opinions particularly between the CDU and the CSU, but it was more serious than previously.

The opinions held by members of the opposition varied too much for it to be possible to divide those that held them into 'doves', who would be prepared under certain circumstances to comply with the government's policy, and 'hawks', who rejected it outright whatever the terms of the Eastern treaties. Between these poles there was a whole range of attitudes, and a number of factors complicated the picture still further.

First, the views of individuals and groups did change during the course of the opposition period. It is sometimes difficult to tell how far these fluctuations of opinion were based on conviction and to what extent they were influenced by the need to placate elements within the party or were made for public consumption. Rainer Barzel, a politician with a reputation for suiting the word to the tactic, used fundamentalist language when the occasion demanded it, yet chose to resign his position as *Fraktion* leader in May 1973 on a matter of principle, namely the vote of CDU/CSU Bundestag deputies opposing UN entry against his own advice. In a statement read to the CDU Federal Committee on 12 May, Barzel warned that *'Wir müssen den Anschluss an die Weltpolitik finden'* — that his party must learn to come to terms with the reality of the international situation.

Secondly, opposition leaders sometimes appeared to contradict their own positions. Bruno Heck, the CDU General Secretary, lectured his party at the Mainz Congress in November 1969 on the need to accept the fact that the new Brandt government had the right of policy initiative; yet just a month before he had issued a memorandum to party members forecasting a period of political ambiguity: 'This applies above all to the field of Eastern and German policy; in domestic policy mistakes committed may be revised, but wrong developments in foreign policy cannot be made good.'[6] Heck later took a fairly adamant stand against *Ostpolitik*.

The third complicating factor was that the CDU/CSU's concrete objections to *Ostpolitik* were continually overtaken by events. The feeling that the opposition had to search for new objections whenever Brandt scored a treaty success was reinforced when Barzel returned from a visit to Moscow in December 1971. On this occasion, he gave a press conference in which he announced that his party still disapproved of the treaty with the Soviet Union because Moscow did not accept the European Community. This objection ceased to have any validity when, two months later, Brezhnev expressed *de facto* recognition of the EEC.

The government's breakthrough in *Ostpolitik* from 1970 onwards, and the pace at which it pursued negotiations, forced the opposition to stand up and be counted. *Ostpolitik* could no longer be viewed as an abstract debating issue. The opposition, due to its stronger negative tendencies, found itself pushed by the speed of events more and more into the *Neinsager-Ecke* (the 'no' corner), while its specific objections to the various treaties assumed more fundamentalist overtones. With these general points in mind, it is now possible to categorise the members of the CDU/CSU according to their differing attitudes to *Ostpolitik*.

1   *Absolute opponents of* Ostpolitik *in principle*

This large group may be termed the *Ordnungszelle* school of thought, since its core was the CSU and its viewpoint reflected the historical role of Bavarian conservatives in upholding 'traditional' German values — with particular emphasis on the need to combat Communism. The belief that Chancellor Brandt was on the road to 'appeasement' was frequently expressed in the speeches of CSU leaders, most notably by Baron von Guttenberg, who saw *Ostpolitik* as the fulfilment of the aims of Soviet totalitarianism. Alfons Goppel, the Bavarian Minister-President, remarked in a speech at Grafenwöhr in November 1972 that 'if developments go any further, we shall have reunification from the other side'. This principled objection to *Ostpolitik* found its crudest expression in the pages of the *Bayernkurier* (the CSU organ), which, at the time that Brandt took office in 1969, featured a large banner headline referring to him as 'The Sell-Out Chancellor'. Such alarmist predictions were often coupled with warnings about the danger of 'Socialism' within the Federal Republic itself. This reactionary attitude towards *Ostpolitik* – aptly called the 'Adenauer reflex' by the playwright Martin Walser, who recognised a tendency to refer back to the rigid policies that Adenauer had adopted towards the Soviet Union in the 1950s – was not confined to the CSU. Alfred Dregger, the chairman of the CDU in Hesse, followed the CSU line in seeing the Basic Treaty with the GDR as 'the crowning of the Russians' *Westpolitik*'. The fundamentalist rejection of Ostpolitik was evident at different levels of the party structure: within the parliamentary party, it was particularly evident among CSU deputies and the refugee elements, as well as among deputies from certain rural areas; and, within the regional branches *(Landesverbände)* of the CDU, it was most noticeable in Hesse and, to a lesser degree, Baden-Württemberg. The impression gained from interviews with CDU activists at the regional and local levels during 1972–73 was that a principled opposition to *Ostpolitik* had been built into the party's belief system. This sometimes followed from a general sympathy with Strauss's ideas, especially in certain rural areas outside Bavaria.

2   Conservative opponents

Whereas the first group were reactionary in their attitude to *Ostpolitik,* and were not prepared to give any ground, this second group were less fossilised in their attitudes. They expressed concern about continuity with the *Ostpolitik* that the CDU had initiated while in office, and complained that Brandt was moving too fast in his accommodation with the Soviet bloc. The obvious spokesman for this group was Gerhard Schröder, the former Foreign Minister and architect of the commercial *Ostpolitik* of the mid-1960s. He spoke of his fears about Social Democratic illusions in the face of 'Soviet hardness' and advocated the need for greater 'realism' in *Ostpolitik*. Schröder's views were broadly held by such CDU leaders as Werner Marx, the Bundestag *Fraktion* spokesman on foreign affairs, and Gerhard Stoltenberg, the party's economic affairs spokesman and, later, Minister-President in Schleswig-Holstein.

Sometimes the dividing line between these two categories was unclear.

Various party leaders fluctuated between total opposition to particular treaties and a more flexible approach on other occasions. Dr Kiesinger, who remained CDU Chairman for the first two years in opposition, showed himself more in agreement with the principled opponents, particularly in the months following his loss of the Chancellorship. He deplored Brandt's failure, in the government declaration of October 1969, to make the traditional reference to the Federal Republic's claim to represent the whole of the German nation. This second group might be said also to include. the 'flexible fundamentalists', those opposition politicians who made absolutist statements in public, but in practice kept their options open.

3 Rational or conditional critics

This group argued in terms of a balance of advantage. They indicated a certain sympathy with *Ostpolitik* in principle, but protested that Brandt had not negotiated realistically. He had given away too much too readily. The best representative of this attitude was Richard von Weizsäcker, who rose to prominence after the CDU had gone into opposition. His viewpoint is illustrated by an article he wrote for *Die Zeit* in November 1970; this was reasoned, balanced, and free of the emotional catchphrases typical of the fundamentalist opponents. Weizsäcker was concerned that the *Ostpolitik* could be exploited by the Soviet Union to promote the disintegration of the West, and advocated more effort towards achieving political unity in Western Europe. He concluded by saying that polarisation over foreign policy could have dangerous consequences.[7]

4 The positive element

This small minority not only agreed in principle with the *Ostpolitik,* but also generally went along with Brandt's actual policy of negotiating treaties with different countries of the Eastern bloc. It was not very influential inside the Bundestag *Fraktion* and included the handful of deputies like Walter Leisler Kiep who in 1973 voted for the ratification of the Basic Treaty with the GDR. Kiep took an independent line in the CDU by maintaining in public that one must be realistic and come to terms with the changed international situation, particularly as the *Ostpolitik* had support from the Western powers.[8] This readiness to accept both the *Ostpolitik* and its consequences was more evident at other levels of the party, above all in the CDU's youth organisation, the Young Union.

The views of the positive element became more respected after the opposition lost the 1972 Bundestag election, but during the first period of opposition they were submerged due to the balance of argument within the party being heavily weighted in favour of the negative groups. An additional factor here was the CDU/CSU's good performance in the *Land* elections in the early 1970s:[9] this misled the party into thinking that its approach had public support. In reality, the CDU/CSU was prevented from taking a convincing and tenable stand on *Ostpolitik* because of its internal divisions. The Christian Democrats were torn between reality and their traditional outlook, and simply reacted to events as they occurred. As Walter Leisler Kiep commented, with reference to the opposition's abstention in the Bundestag vote on the Moscow and Warsaw treaties in May 1972, 'The CDU could not say "yes" because, in the case of a large part of the *Fraktion,* a complete assessment of the work of the treaty did not allow that. It could not say "no" because the damage resulting from a rejection seemed too great.'[10]

There was a strong tactical flavour to the opposition's position on *Ostpolitik*, for this was determined to a significant degree by the party's internal situation. This aspect will now be discussed in relation to the effect of the *Ostpolitik* debate on the party itself.

It can be said at once that the *Ostpolitik* debate had a considerable effect on the CDU/CSU, since it crystallised certain problems, relating to the party's structure and character, that became magnified in opposition. The party was singularly unprepared for the role of opposition, for its basic outlook had been conditioned by its experience as the major national governing party, a position that it had enjoyed for twenty years from the inception of the Federal Republic. Not only did its leaders resent the fact that they could no longer claim the right of policy-making, but, in addition, the party itself had made only slow progress towards becoming a mass party in the organisational sense: for the first ten years at least, the party machine had been neglected due to Adenauer's prestige as a national and international figure. Furthermore, foreign policy itself had, particularly during the 1950s, acted as an integrating factor in the CDU/CSU. Adenauer, with his overriding concern for foreign, and especially European, policy, had chosen to link party solidarity in this field with allegiance to himself as party leader. As Arnold Heidenheimer has written, with reference to German rearmament and European integration, 'Those within the party who were critical of the Chancellor on domestic questions found themselves left with little choice but to close ranks in support of a policy to which he was absolutely determined to commit the party's fortunes.'[11] Due to Adenauer's precedent, there developed a marked association between strong leadership of the party and a firm and united stand on foreign policy. It is significant that the mutterings over Ludwig Erhard's weak leadership, during his period as Chancellor in the mid-1960s, should have been expressed above all in the form of party divisions on the questions of the Western Alliance and the nature of a united Europe. An added reason for the CDU/CSU's difficulty in adjusting to the new situation, in which *Ostpolitik* became the dominant issue, was that the party had been brought up on a staple diet of *Westpolitik*. This, combined with the party's anti-Communism, accounted for the rigidity of its attitudes, which increasingly pushed it in a direction that seemed unrealistic. The lack of cohesiveness in the CDU did not help either, for as Rüdiger Göb, the party's executive manager, commented, in complaining that too many people in the CDU were making their own policies, 'The opposition is still like an automobile that is being driven by several motorists at one time. One is doing the steering, another has his foot on the accelerator, a third is pumping the brakes and yet another is operating the indicator.'[12] By comparison with the SPD, the CDU suffered from a relatively low degree of international party discipline, stemming from the pluralistic and federalistic nature of its internal relationships.

These background factors contribute much to an understanding of the internal problems faced by the opposition during the *Ostpolitik* debate. The effects that this had on the party will now be viewed from three angles: the relationship between party attitudes to *Ostpolitik* and the leadership question; the *Ostpolitik* issue as a divisive factor within the opposition, both between the CDU and the CSU and within the CDU itself; and the effect of *Ostpolitik* on the party's credibility.

Just as *Ostpolitik* was the predominant issue during the early 1970s, so the leadership problem remained fairly prominent during the same period. Relevant to the coincidence of these two questions was the fact that the CDU had in the past, and particularly in the 1950s, successfully managed to compensate for its structural weaknesses by its emphasis on the charisma of the party leader. In opposition, the CDU lacked a sovereign figure at its head, for the establised prestige of the Chancellorship could no longer be counted in its favour. Although Dr Kiesinger had been re-elected CDU Chairman in November 1969, he had lost face because he was no longer Chancellor, and it was accepted as unlikely that he would reappear as the party's standard-bearer in a future Bundestag election. The leadership was therefore effectively open once the party had gone into opposition. Barzel exploited his position as parliamentary spokesman of the opposition and eventually emerged as CDU Chairman in the autumn of 1971. A few months later he was chosen as the party's candidate for the post of Chancellor, so that the leadership question was officially closed; but in practice it was never solved satisfactorily. [13] Barzel's authority within the party as a whole was limited, and his position was frequently undermined by the machinations of Strauss. His steps as party leader were dogged by the *Ostpolitik* factor, for the issue was centrally related to the major internal problems he encountered: first, how to keep the party united when *Ostpolitik* proved so divisive; and, secondly, how to prevent his party rivals and opponents from exploiting the issue to weaken his leadership.

The difficulties involved in Barzel's attempt to save face and preserve some semblance of party unity are illustrated by the opposition's reaction to the final stage in the negotiation of the Moscow Treaty in August 1970. The CDU was presented with a *fait accompli* by the government and required to pronounce on the matter. A ready statement was not forthcoming. For a couple of weeks the opposition remained officially silent, but its predicament was aggravated when several of its leaders revealed their own opinions of the treaty, apparently without proper consultation with their colleagues. CSU leaders and Kiesinger wanted to condemn the treaty outright; Richard Stücklen, Chairman of the CSU group within the *Fraktion*, even rejected the treaty without reading its text. Other CDU leaders warned against an over-hasty condemnation. Barzel did manage to push through a compromise position at a meeting of the party praesidium, but with great effort, for half of the four-hour meeting was spent in working out the communiqué for the press. [14] This attempt to paper over the cracks was so transparent that it could be only temporarily effective, and differences within the party reappeared in public on later occasions. Initial reactions to the Berlin Agreement concluded in September 1971 ranged from open acceptance by Heinrich Köppler, chairman of the Rhineland CDU, through qualified or conditional approval by some CDU leaders, to outright defiance by the CSU. The opposition's hydra-headed public position on the *Ostpolitik* issue simply served to underline the fact that Barzel was not master of his own party. This became painfully obvious during the ratification process in May 1972, when Barzel attempted to bring his party round to voting in favour of the Moscow and Warsaw treaties after working out an agreed formula with the government for a declaration on the aims of West German foreign policy. He did not succeed because he switched his position too suddenly, without having educated his party to take a more positive stand. Barzel was forced by pressures from within the opposition (especially from the CSU) to back down in public in favour of an

54

abstention vote. This, coming as this did after Barzel's failure, in the constructive vote of no-confidence the previous month, to replace Brandt as Chancellor, had harmful consequences for his leadership. Barzel never succeeded in getting off the hook on *Ostpolitik*, for the issue continued to check his persistent efforts to forge a real party unity.

Any analysis of the *Ostpolitik* as a divisive factor among the Christian Democrats must start off by recognising that the opposition really consisted of two political parties, each with its own chairman, structured organisation, and membership. The CSU had a number of advantages, such as greater cohesion, a more efficient organisation, and a charismatic figure as its leader; and this allowed it to exert pressure on the CDU when it came to differences over *Ostpolitik*. The strengths of the CSU reinforced significantly the negative orientation of the whole opposition on this issue. Barzel's dilemma during the ratification crisis of May 1972 was above all due to Strauss's change of mind about the treaties, a development that set in motion the pressures operating against Barzel's wish to create bipartisanship on the treaties. The opposition's decision to abstain facilitated the passage of the treaties, but did not erase the ill feelings colouring relations between the two parties and between fundamentalist and moderate elements within the CDU. This conflict erupted in a more violent way after the defeat in the 1972 Bundestag election, when Strauss threatened to withdraw his party from the common *Fraktion* of the CDU and CSU. He made rejection of the Basic Treaty with the GDR one of the main conditions for a continuation of the combined opposition. Thus, the *Ostpolitik* issue, particularly as it was such an emotive question, served to bring to the surface differences that already existed inside the CDU/CSU. The extent to which these differences were aired in public was also enhanced by changes that had been occurring in the CDU since the late 1960s — in particular a slow trend towards internal party debate. This had first been demonstrated by the formulation of the Berlin Programme of 1968.

The effect of the *Ostpolitik* on the CDU/CSU's credibility must be measured in the light of Barzel's ultimate intention as opposition leader: to counteract the possibility that the CDU/CSU might, in its new role, lose its aura of political respectability as basically a governing party. The party's antics over *Ostpolitik* did, however, do a great deal to undermine its image, particularly as pressures within the CDU/CSU drove it in a direction opposite to that of public opinion. Some CDU leaders were aware of this danger. On 10 January 1972, Konrad Kraske, newly appointed as CDU General Secretary by Barzel, sent a confidential memorandum to executive managers in the *Landesverbände*, saying that:

The CDU has neither the motive nor the intention of postponing the ratification process of the Eastern treaties. It must, on the contrary, be interested in seeing the arguments over the treaties concluded by the summer, so that, in the event of the acceptance of the treaties, the time remaining until the election can be used to design a new strategy (the main points: European unification, inner German relations, and the alleviation of human problems). In spite of the topicality of foreign political questions, domestic policy must remain our field and must largely determine the exchanges with our opponents at the latest from the summer of 1972.[15]

The opposition's dilemma re-emerged during the Bundestag election campaign in autumn 1972, for the conclusion of the Basic Treaty with the GDR only ten days before polling day raised the governing coalition's chances of re-election and caught the headlines for the remainder of the campaign. It also exposed to full public view the weaknesses of the opposition's position on *Ostpolitik*. Barzel found himself in an awkward situation and was once again forced to sit on the fence, though this time his behaviour was even less plausible than before. As opposition leader he was required to criticise (which, simply on account of the party's internal situation, meant that he had to phrase his criticisms in a principled way), and yet he still had to budget for the possibility that he might find himself Chancellor and therefore forced to take the situation as it came when he entered office. The Basic Treaty did more than any other issue to discredit the opposition's chances during the campaign. [16] The negative impact that the party's line on *Ostpolitik* had on its performance in the election was confirmed by post-election reports from the *Landesverbände*. In March 1973, the CDU's Rhineland branch stressed that the party's stance had cost it credibility: 'The Union did not understand how to present to the voters, in a convincing manner, its indisputable readiness to accept peace and *détente* ... with different statements coming from well-known Union politicians, the impression of unconditional rejection was bound to be created.'[17]

The outlook for the future, now that the CDU/CSU has suffered a decisive electoral defeat and is well into its second period of opposition, is different — if only because the *Ostpolitik* debate is effectively over and the government is paying more attention to domestic politics, particularly since Schmidt became Chancellor. The CDU/CSU realised that it had antagonised the electorate, who still felt a distaste for bitter partisan conflict, on an issue widely regarded as popular. Now the party does seem to have got itself off the hook on *Ostpolitik*. This has been facilitated by the change in the opposition leadership. Barzel's replacement as *Fraktion* chairman by Karl Carstens, and, even more significantly, Helmut Kohl's assumption of the CDU Chairmanship in June 1973, reflected a widespread desire within the opposition to make a fresh start. Carstens has continued to follow a conservative line whenever foreign policy issues have arisen, and has not shown any special aptitude for domestic affairs; but Kohl possesses the advantage of having avoided deep involvement in the party's internal conflicts over *Ostpolitik*. He was able to achieve this convenient position through his status as provincial party leader in the Rhineland-Palatinate, where he was not required to take any strong line on international matters. Kohl was fortunate in that when he took over from Barzel as CDU Chairman the *Ostpolitik* issue had virtually subsided. He was thus able to concentrate his party's attention more on social and economic issues, as is shown by his speeches to the CDU congresses at Bonn in June 1973 and at Hamburg in November of that year. Kohl's line is that the Eastern treaties have now become a fact of political life, although one should not harbour any illusions about Soviet intentions. As he said at the congress of the West Berlin CDU in April 1973, 'The treaties have created a new situation — one must come to terms with this, but also make sure that the treaties are not exploited by the other side'. [18] Kohl's appointment of Walter Leisler Kiep as foreign policy spokesman of the CDU praesidium suggested not so much an agreement with Kiep's independent views on *Ostpolitik* as a willingness to allow more flexibility in this policy area.

The CDU/CSU opposition's *de facto* acceptance of Brandt's policy must finally be related to its adjustment to the role of opposition, for the result of the 1972 Bundestag election underlined that its chances of a return to power had to be long-term rather than short-term. Chancellor Schmidt's own sceptical attitude towards *Ostpolitik* has helped to narrow the once wide gulf between the positions of the two main West German parties on this issue. The CDU/CSU's reaction to Brandt's *Ostpolitik* initiatives during the period 1970–73 must, however, be judged in the context of the difficulties the party experienced in adapting to the unaccustomed role of opposition, a problem that was heightened by its long experience in government, its loose organisational structure, and the absence of strong internal party discipline. This problem was further complicated by the tendency of opposition politics in West Germany to assume a fundamentalist character.

Notes

[1] Ralf Dahrendorf, *Society and Democracy in Germany,* London 1968.

[2] Quoted in *Die Zeit,* 17 April 1970.

[3] In response to opposition interjections about the rate of inflation, Alex Möller, the Federal Finance Minister, remarked, 'Those who bore responsibility for these world wars and the inflations that followed them are nearer in spirit to you than to the Social Democrats.' Möller was presenting the government's budget for 1971. Opposition deputies reacted by withdrawing from the chamber of the Bundestag, and saying that in his speech the Minister had 'disqualified himself as a democrat'.

[4] See Otto Kirchheimer, 'Germany: the vanishing opposition' in Robert A. Dahl, *Political Oppositions in Western Democracies,* 1966.

[5] *Die Zeit,* 10 December 1971.

[6] Bruno Heck, memorandum to CDU members, 4 October 1969.

[7] *Die Zeit,* 6 November 1970.

[8] See Walter Leisler Kiep's justification of his vote in favour of the Basic Treaty with the GDR in *Frankfurter Allgemeine,* 12 May 1973.

[9] See the discussion of this in Geoffrey Pridham, 'A "nationalization" process. Federal politics and state elections in West Germany' in *Government and Opposition,* Autumn 1973, pp.455–72.

[10] Interview in *Die Zeit,* 1 December 1973.

[11] Arnold Heidenheimer, 'Foreign policy and party discipline in the CDU' in *Parliamentary Affairs,* 1959–60.

[12] *Stuttgarter Zeitung,* 30 August 1971.

[13] See Geoffrey Pridham, 'The CDU/CSU opposition in West Germany, 1969–1972: A party in search of an organization' in *Parliamentary Affairs,* Spring 1973.

[14] *Süddeutsche Zeitung,* 28 August 1970.

[15] Konrad Kraske to CDU *Landesgeschäftsführer,* 10 January 1972.

[16] See Ludolf Eltermann, Helmut Jung and Werner Kaltefleiter, 'Drei Fragen zur Bundestagswahl 1972' in *Aus Politik und Zeitgeschichte,* 17 November 1973. According to this study, even a high proportion of CDU voters viewed *Ostpolitik* positively, and consequently many of these people tended to divorce themselves from the party's stand on this issue.

[17] Report of the Rhineland *Landesverband* of the CDU on the 1972 Bundestag election, March 1973.

[18] *Süddeutsche Zeitung,* 9 April 1973.

3   The Ostpolitik and Domestic Politics in East Germany

David CHILDS

Before trying to evaluate the GDR's response to the challenge of *Ostpolitik*, we must examine three things: first, the historical development of the GDR; secondly, the leadership of the GDR – the individuals responsible for dealing with West German initiatives; and, thirdly, the figures showing the growth of contacts between the citizens of the two Germanies, for such contacts could greatly affect the development of the GDR.

Until well into the 1960s, the GDR, compared with its neighbours on both sides of the ideological frontier, was in many respects a sad place indeed.[1] Though there was no unemployment and no real poverty, and though living standards were rising and compared favourably with those of the other Warsaw Pact states, the people felt cheated because their brothers in the Federal Republic were clearly better off.[2] There were many educational and cultural opportunities,[3] but life, with a regimented culture and a mass media which was centrally controlled in line with official ideology, seemed dull. For news and entertainment many people turned to the West German media, while many writers – Uwe Johnson, Christa Reinig and Manfred Bieler among them – gave up security in the GDR for freedom in the Federal Republic. The people were harassed and harangued into doing 'voluntary' social and political work of all kinds, and there seemed little time for quiet relaxation and private pleasures. The relatively poor living standards and the lack of private life were among the main reasons for the mass exodus from the GDR before August 1961.

The East German régime strove hard to convince its citizens of its legitimacy, but many remained sceptical.[4] Its obsequious stance *vis à vis* not only anything Soviet, but also anything Russian in the broader sense, lessened its chances of acceptance, and seemed irrelevant to its main objectives. It never dared seek legitimacy through elections involving a genuine choice, and, on the international front, it was legitimised only by the recognition accorded it by the Warsaw Pact states, Cuba, Yugoslavia and the Asian Communist states. These were states that carried little weight with the average East German. Moreover, the Soviet Union had, in effect, legitimised Bonn by recognising it in 1955, but the Western powers refused to recognise Russia's client. This certainly affected the régime's standing among the people, and affected the party cadres psychologically. East German officials had a sense of inferiority and insecurity unknown elsewhere in Eastern Europe after 1956. The rising of 1953[5] and the debunking of Stalin in 1956 destroyed the faith and idealism of the new generation of party cadres in the GDR, and their régime's continued international isolation, together with the siren calls from Bonn, put a great strain on their loyalty. In the other countries of the Eastern bloc, comrades could argue that, since theirs were the only internationally recognised régimes for their respective countries, they should try to reform them from within. To leave would be treachery to the national cause. The GDR cadres could not use this argument with the same conviction. They had to consider whether they could do better for themselves, and more for their country, by going to the Federal Republic, which claimed to speak for the whole of the German nation.

The building of the Berlin Wall in August 1961 forced many to make up their minds quickly and ended the uncertainty. The sense of shame, disgust and impotent anger that many functionaries, together with the mass of ordinary East Germans, felt soon gave way to resignation and, then, a determination to make the best of things. This determination, combined with the introduction of the New Economic System in 1963, appear to have been among the key factors that caused a considerable improvement in life in the Democratic Republic in the 1960s.[6] Having built the Wall, the régime decided that it too had to make compromises, and a mild thaw took place in the cultural life of the GDR, especially between 1962 and 1965.[7] Because of these trends and the country's Olympic successes and achievements in education, the GDR's standing in the world improved.[8] Western observers believed that the régime was at last consolidating itself, and there was even mention of the growth of a distinctive GDR consciousness.[9] Nevertheless, international recognition continued to evade the GDR, despite closer ties with the Arab states and Ulbricht's much-publicised visit to Nasser in 1965.

Internally, two things remained unchanged in the GDR as the 1960s drew to a close: the large Soviet garrison and the man at the top, Walter Ulbricht.[10] Ulbricht had shown a remarkable capacity for survival. In 1950, he became General Secretary, and, later, First Secretary, of the SED, having been the key man among German Communists long before the GDR was set up in 1949. Stalin's death and dethronement did not affect his position, nor did the later upheavals in the Soviet bloc —

including the downfall of Khrushchev in 1964, and the rise and fall of Dubcek in 1968. By the time that he, as the official version still has it, asked to be relieved of the secretaryship in 1971, the GDR had been recognised by a number of non-Communist states. When he died in office as head of state in 1973, international recognition of the German Democratic Republic had been largely achieved. By that time, however, Ulbricht had been dead politically for some time.

The signs of Ulbricht's political demise were the lack of publicity given to him as head of state, and the speed with which he ceased to be a source of inspiration to party speech writers. Up to his fall, at least one reference to his wisdom had been mandatory in all speeches; now it is Honecker who pours forth the golden words. When Ulbricht died in August 1973, it took his colleagues forty-eight days to bury his ashes in the *Gedenkstätte der Sozialisten* in Friedrichsfelde (Berlin). Compare this with the speed with which the King of Sweden was dispatched — ten days! Yet the Swedish monarch was honoured by official mourners from all over the world. No foreign politician, diplomat, or other representative was mentioned as present at Ulbricht's funeral. This must have been due more to an East German reluctance to invite anyone than to a foreign boycott of the dead leader. Remarkably, in these circumstances, the first anniversary of Ulbricht's death was mentioned in the East German press. A delegation from the Central Committee of the SED laid a wreath in Friedrichsfelde. The only full members of the Politburo in the delegation were Hermann Axen and Paul Verner, both reckoned as close to Honecker. The smallness of the delegation would seem to suggest that the commemorative ceremony was just a matter of form, a fulsome attempt to emphasise continuity of policy. But what about continuity of leadership? Are the heirs to the Ulbricht inheritance really as united as they would have us believe? There is some evidence that they are not.

Human nature being what it is, one would expect rivalry between the Saarlander Erich Honecker and the Berliner Willi Stoph. Stoph (born 1914) has been prominent in the public eye for much longer than Honecker (born 1912). As Chairman of the Council of Ministers *(Ministerrat)* from 1964, he was second only to Ulbricht in public order of precedence. He has had enormous experience in different sectors of GDR life, having at one time been in charge of basic industries, and, later, Minister of the Interior (1952—55) and Minister of Defence (1956—60). His occupation of the last two posts would indicate a high degree of trust on the part of the Soviets. As Chairman of the Council of Ministers, he was somewhat more popular than Honecker, who was too closely identified with the party, the government being more popular with the public than the SED. Honecker could resent this. Stoph could argue that he, and not Honecker, was best qualified to be first man in the land; even in the Politburo, Stoph has been a full member for longer than Honecker. Honecker, on the other hand, can claim moral superiority by virtue of the ten years he spent behind bars under Hitler. Stoph claims that he took part in 'illegal anti-Fascist activity' in the Third Reich, but he did not suffer imprisonment. Honecker, as a man of limited formal education and no special expertise, could resent that Stoph, while no expert himself, was surrounded by experts in the Council of Ministers.

Since Erich Honecker took over as First Secretary of the SED (Socialist Unity Party), one notes constitutional and leadership changes, as well as an even greater emphasis on the leading role of the party. All these changes strongly suggest an attempt by Honecker to build up his own position. At the time when Ulbricht was confirmed as Chairman of the Council of State *(Staatsrat),* that body, set up in 1960 on the death of President Pieck, lost some of its influence. The Council of Ministers, on the other hand, was upgraded in October 1972, at which time Stoph was still its Chairman. He was demoted a year later to the Chairmanship of the Council of State. This happened two months after Ulbricht's death.

The man who replaced Stoph in the upgraded Council of Ministers is generally regarded as a Honecker man. Horst Sindermann, born in 1915, was formerly the SED leader in the important industrial region of Halle. In May 1971 he was made Stoph's deputy in the Council of Ministers. Another Honecker associate who gained promotion is Werner Lamberz. Lamberz, now forty-five years old, started life as a heating engineer, and became the Brandenburg secretary of the FDJ (the SED's youth organisation) before studying at the Komsomol High School in Moscow in 1952–53. He then worked his way up through the SED organisation. He is now a full member of the Politburo and is very often just behind Honecker. Other Honecker men have advanced to lesser positions, and it appears that they are poised to take over the Politburo when the old guard go. Honecker is waiting for the retirement of such veterans as Friedrich Ebert, an octogenarian and a former Social Democrat; trade-union leader Herbert Warnke (seven-three years old); ex-USA emigrant Albert Norden (seventy-one); Spanish Civil War veteran Alfred Neumann (sixty-six); and ideologue Kurt Hager (sixty-three), who after fighting in Spain, lived in England for some time. Recently promoted to the Politburo is sixty-four year old General Karl-Heinz Hoffmann, Minister of Defence. Apart from Sindermann and Lamberz, Honecker can already count on Hermann Axen and Paul Verner, both of whom began their party careers as functionaries in the FDJ.

In addition to being known or likely sympathisers of Honecker, those who are promoted tend to be officials rather than experts in economics. Thus the trend towards replacing all-round SED functionaries with experts who are less dogma-oriented (a phenomenon analysed by Professor Ludz and other Western experts) [11] has been halted. Günter Mittag, regarded in the West as the personification of the 'expert trend', has received a setback, and looks somewhat lonely in the Politburo. He has managed, however, to remain a deputy chairman of the Council of Ministers under Horst Sindermann. To sum up, the Secretariats of the Central Committee of the SED, which greatly influence the Council of Ministers, are now as Joachim Nawrocki has pointed out, [12] almost entirely made up of 'ideologues and dogmatists'. In the Politburo itself, twelve out of sixteen members belong to the older, pre-war generation of working-class functionaries. On the other hand though, almost all the candidates for promotion belong to the post-war generation. Their experience and qualifications (often *Diplom-Gesellschaftswissenschaft,* a sort of Marxist sociology degree) mark them out as party functionaries first, with everything else a long way behind. It is these men who are deciding how the GDR will meet the challenge of *Ostpolitik* within its frontiers.

Finally, before leaving the question of the SED's leadership, one point needs to be underlined. Despite the relative weakening in the position of Willi Stoph, it must not be assumed that he is likely to leave the stage (other than by natural causes) in the near future. He has received much publicity as head of state, and is usually put second only to Honecker in order of precedence. In other words, he ranks above Horst Sindermann. Photographs of a very fit-looking Stoph were given much publicity on his sixtieth birthday. A highly flattering letter of congratulation was sent to him by the Central Committee of the party, and on the same day it was announced that the Russians had decided to honour him with the Order of Lenin. This was for his contribution to the development of GDR–Soviet relations. The following day, an almost complete turnout of the Politburo watched Erich Honecker present him with the Karl-Marx Order, the GDR's highest. Herr Stoph received still more publicity when he was reported as having been presented with the Order of Lenin by his Soviet counterpart, Nikolai Podgorny, in Moscow later that month. Thus in its pattern of leadership, as in so much else, the GDR is sticking to the Soviet model of a triumverate.

A very important aspect of the *Ostpolitik,* potentially of great importance for the internal development of the GDR, has been the easing of contacts between the populations of the GDR and the Federal Republic. According to figures released by Brandt in February 1974, the number of West Germans visiting the GDR had increased by 60 per cent since the traffic agreement between the two German states came into operation in October 1972. From October 1972 to the end of 1973, over 2·5 million West Germans visited East Germany, and nearly 53,000 East Germans under retirement age were able to enter the Federal Republic on pressing family matters. [13] Many thousands of East German pensioners crossed the frontier, as was the case before the agreement. In addition, there was a great increase in the number of West Berlin residents going to East Berlin. Other West Germans were able to cross the GDR frontier, due to an agreement under which those living in the frontier zone of the Federal Republic are allowed to visit the area of the GDR adjacent to them. Many of these West Germans and West Berliners were no doubt former GDR citizens who had left East Germany illegally. Since the passing of the Citizenship Law of 16 October 1972, they are no longer regarded as citizens of the GDR and are free from prosecution. One wonders what reports of life in the West they gave to their relatives, friends, and former colleagues in East Germany, and how the East Germans responded to their reports. More will be said about this below.

On examining the party leaders' speeches and the propaganda line taken by the mass media, five themes stand out as the SED's response to the challenge posed by Bonn's *Ostpolitik*. First, great stress is put on the importance — the primacy one could almost say — of ideology, and on ideological rearmament. This is an important aspect of *Abgrenzung*. Secondly, the importance of total unity with, and commitment to, the Soviet Union is underlined again and again. Thirdly, the need for the security organs and the armed forces to remain vigilant is a popular theme. Fourthly, the propaganda value of the continuing battle for prosperity is not neglected. Finally, it is always stressed that this prosperity is to be obtained by an intensification in the building of Socialism/Communism.

In their concern for ideology, the party spokesmen make a number of basic points. One of these is the need for an aggressive strategy in mass political work. [14] Another oft-repeated theme is that peaceful coexistence does not mean ideological coexistence, let alone any kind of convergence of opposing ideologies. On the contrary, because the imperialists dare not launch military aggression, they seek to achieve their ends by ideological subversion. Thus the struggle on the ideological front is intensified. [15] Part and parcel of this imperialist ideological aggression is the use of the ideas of social democracy — 'democratic Socialism' — Trotskyism, Maoism and revisionism to weaken the Socialist camp. [16] DEFA, the East German film company, obviously thinks it has a role to play in countering 'pseudo-Left ideology'. It has recently released a feature film entitled *Wolz. Leben und*

Verklärung eines deutschen Anarchisten, which deals with anarchism and the German Left after 1918; reviewers have been quick to point out that it is highly relevant to the present political situation. Another aspect of this Western ideological offensive is, according to the SED, anti-Soviet agitation; the campaign of Alexander Solzhenitsyn and his backers is considered a key example. The SED organ *Neues Deutschland,* in its issue of 10 January 1974, called *The Gulag Archipelago* 'a stink-bomb against the relaxation' of tensions. The very long article on the book did not actually tell its readers what *Gulag* was about. Nor did it mention the fact that the West German writer Heinrich Böll was one of Solzhenitsyn's supporters. Böll of course, has, in the past received lavish praise in both the Soviet Union and the GDR.

One of Ulbricht's 'crimes' in his last years of power was that he took up a slightly more independent line *vis à vis* the Soviet Union. Honecker cannot be accused on this. After his visit to Moscow in June 1974, it was announced that relations between the two states were going to be closer still, and the citizens of the GDR were reminded that friendship and co-operation with the Soviet Union and the other Socialist states was the basis for the GDR's successful development.[17] The East German leaders are not content just with political unity or growing economic integration with the USSR; they want an even greater orientation towards the Soviet Union in the arts and education as well. Great stress is put on the work of the German-Soviet Friendship Society, and on such things as how many East Germans have seen Soviet films in their local cinemas.[18]

As regards the SED's continued emphasis on vigilance, one need only mention the fact that, in addition to General Hoffmann joining the Politburo, his colleague Mielke, head of the East German security service, has been elevated to candidate membership of the same body. That the security organs are responding to the challenge posed by millions of Western visitors is indicated by the fact that, from June 1972 to March 1974, forty-eight individuals were sentenced by East German courts for helping GDR citizens to cross the frontier illegally.[19] On occasion, the East German press gives great publicity to such prosecutions, and attempts are made to prove that official West Berlin or West German organisations are involved.[20] Cases are also known of the People's Police questioning young people about their contacts with Western visitors to the GDR, and attempts have been made to get them to break off such contacts.[21] This is the practical implication of the theory of *Abgrenzung,* that West Germans and East Germans have little in common in spite of their common language and common past.

In their struggle to raise living standards and thereby satisfy their people, the East German leaders know that they have no easy task. The fact is, that, despite the *Abgrenzung* propaganda, the average East German still measures himself against what he knows his brother or cousin is able to do with his earnings in West Germany. The SED has recently been helped somewhat by the amount of discussion on Western television, which so many East Germans watch, about inflation, the energy crisis, the threat of unemployment, and the other economic ills of the Western world. The GDR press has not been slow to exploit this opportunity. Unfortunately, however, West Germany is still doing better than most, so that the SED leaders cannot relax their efforts to satisfy their people. In one area that is, by now, a traditional cause of friction between the East Germans and their rulers they can do but little. This is the demand that more and more East Germans are making for foreign travel. It is still virtually impossible for the average GDR citizen to holiday outside the Warsaw Pact states, even in Yugoslavia; and it is occasionally admitted that some of the East European resorts, in Bulgaria for instance, leave a lot to be desired. The international recognition of the GDR has removed one excuse that used to be advanced for not allowing East Germans to travel outside the Soviet bloc. Another area of real difficulty for the GDR leadership is private motoring. East Germany must still be about the most under-motorised industrial state in the world. Whether the recent oil crisis in the West has done anything to weaken the average East German's desire for private transport is doubtful.

In another traditionally difficult area of policy, housing, the GDR press has given great publicity to plans for considerable expansion. In 1975, 93,000 dwellings are planned, and a further 33,000 are due for modernisation. [22] If these plans are fulfilled they will make 1975 the most successful year for housing in the history of the Republic. The last time that targets of this sort were achieved was in 1961, when 85,600 dwellings were completed and a further 6,400 were modernised or reconstructed. In 1973, according to the official figures, 80,725 new dwelling units were completed. [23] Usually the GDR's building industry does not fulfil its planned targets, but apparently it did so in 1973, and in the first half of 1974 it was reported as being on schedule. Welcome though this news is, the GDR will, even if the plans for the next period are realised, be nowhere near solving its housing problem. Much of its housing stock is old, overcrowded, and poorly equipped with basic amenities. According to an official survey taken in 1971, 16·9 per cent of dwellings were constructed prior to 1870, 21·5 per cent belonged to the period 1870–99, and 18·3 per cent had been built between 1900 and 1918. (In 1961, the comparable figures were 21·7, 23·3, and 19·7 per cent

66

respectively.) Thus, the majority of houses and flats in the GDR in 1971 were the products of Imperial Germany! They were appropriately equipped. The great majority of dwellings (3,476,239 out of a total of 5,971,043) did not have indoor toilets, only 2,311,811 enjoyed the luxury of a bath/shower room. 48 per cent consisted of only one or two rooms, while a further 33·5 per cent had three rooms. Only 20·8 per cent of dwellings were of post-war construction.[24]

In the provision of durable consumer goods, further progress was recorded in 1973. By the end of the year, 77 per cent of households had television, 75 per cent possessed refrigerators, and 66 per cent were equipped with washing machines. In 1965, the percentages were 48, 26 and 28 respectively. In this sphere, then, considerable progress has been achieved. Other improvements that have recently been announced are an increase in the minimum holiday from fifteen to eighteen working days (a measure claimed to affect 1·5 million East Germans), improved conditions for shift-workers, increased salaries for white-collar employees, and reductions in the retail prices of women's clothing.[25] These measures, together with the bleak reports from the West, should go some way to placating the mass of East Germans.

One limitation on the ability of the GDR rapidly to improve the living standards of its people stems from its continued commitments to large deliveries to the USSR. It must also export its consumer goods to the West, especially West Germany, with which it at present has a massive trade deficit.

Whether East Germany is gradually catching up with the Federal Republic in terms of living standards is difficult to say. The SED's propagandists no longer talk about catching up with West Germany in this respect. However, they make great play of inflation in the Federal Republic, even though the West Germans suffer less from inflation than most of their neighbours. The GDR certainly made some gains in its race with the Federal Republic as a result of the 1966–67 downturn in the West German economy, but later in the decade these gains were eliminated and the gap may have widened. In 1970–71, the balance probably swung in the direction of the GDR again.[26] Whatever the actual state of play, the East Germans still have a long haul ahead.

It might have been expected that when Honecker at last took over as First Secretary of the SED he would not have introduced any dramatic policy changes, preferring to feel his way first. However, the fact that he had been Ulbricht's heir-apparent for so long perhaps made him impatient to brand his own mark on the body of the GDR. Admittedly, the régime has not changed fundamentally since Erich Honecker took over, but there has been much emphasis on intensifying the development of Socialism.

One of the first practical measures in this direction was the nationalis-ation of many private and partially private (mixed) undertakings. In April 1972, the 'Central Committee [of the SED] decided upon steps for the further development of Socialist production relations, and for the removal of certain symptoms of recapitalisation in the GDR'. [27] At that time the private sector was responsible for about 5·4 per cent of the national income, and the mixed enterprises for about another 9 per cent. Together they employed nearly 2 million adult workers (including office and other staff), as against nearly 6·7 million employed in the fully nationalised and co-operative enterprises. [28] These mixed and private firms were mainly involved in light industries, particularly textiles and food. In 1969, the mixed enterprises alone accounted for 23 per cent of the output of the textile industry, and 20 per cent of the food industry's. Thus they were of considerable importance, the industries themselves having a direct bearing on the standard of living. As they had not been criticised for failing to meet their targets, and as higher living standards were a high priority for SED leaders, it is difficult to understand why the move to nationalise these enterprises was made at this time. Possibly it was a sop to the doctrinaire elements in the SED, meant to reassure them that closer ties with West Germany in no way heralded ideological retreat; or perhaps it was a sop to the workers and poorer members of the intelligentsia, whom one sometimes heard criticising the material privileges of the private manager-owners. Otherwise it could have been meant to display the SED's orthodoxy to the rest of the Eastern bloc, the other states of which are virtually free of private enterprise. Finally, it could simply have been the result of the new First Secretary's desire to demonstrate that he intended to innovate and not merely administer.

Another sign of the increased zeal for catching up with the Soviet Union has been the new emphasis on the use of the word 'Communist' to describe members of the SED. Until recently this was frowned upon, the party having been born of the union of Social Democrats and Communists, a historical event that the SED ('Socialist Unity Party') has tried to exploit in its relations with the West German Social Democrats and other Western Socialists. Honecker used the term 'Communist' in reference to the SED during his closing remarks to the twelfth session of the Central Committee on 5 July 1974. In the same speech, he rather pointedly — one might even suggest, tactlessly — referred to both Ernst Thälmann, the German Communist leader during the Weimar Republic, and Wilhelm Pieck, the figurehead of German Communism after the war, while omitting mention of his own mentor, Walter Ulbricht. Marx and

Engels, and, of course, Lenin and Brezhnev, were mentioned, but not Bebel, Liebknecht and Luxemburg. Thus Honecker severely circumscribed the ideological boundaries of the SED, relating it to the Stalin-dominated party of Thälmann rather than to the earlier, broader movement of German Marxism. Another example of this renewed and very one-sided, emphasis on the experience of the Stalinist Communist Party is a new set of stamps commemorating eight German workers' leaders. Seven stamps depict Communist leaders who served their party faithfully. The odd man out is Otto Grotewohl, the Social Democrat who, in 1946, led the SPD in the Soviet Zone into unity with the Communists. Grotewohl later became head of government in the GDR, and retained the post until his death in 1964.

At the July meeting of the Central Committee referred to above, both Erich Honecker and Hermann Axen seemed to underline more strongly than before the leading role of the working class, meaning the SED. All in all, one can expect that in the near future there will be certain changes in the political forms pertaining in the GDR, with the SED possibly changing its name to include the word 'Communist', and a possible weakening of the allied parties' share in the various administrative and parliamentary bodies. Undoubtedly, such developments would be in keeping with ideological *Abgrenzung,* underlining the GDR's alienation from the Federal Republic and its solidarity with the 'community of Socialist states'.

In apparent contradiction of this 'Left' ideological movement, there have been a number of interesting developments in the cultural life of the GDR since Honecker took charge. As one Western observer of the cultural scene there put it, 'We shall have to revise our received idea of the Other Germany as the land of the squarest of Red squares; at the moment it's a sort of ideological and cultural wonderland, strange to experience, hard to describe, and impossible to analyse confidently.' [29] The justification for these remarks is the unobtrusive rehabilitation of writers like Stefan Heym and Reiner Kunze, the more ambitious plans of East German publishing houses to publish Western authors, and the greater daring of DEFA, the state film corporation. Stefan Heym returned to the GDR from the United States after war service in the US Army. In 1965, he was banned from the GDR's cultural life after writing a book on the 1953 rising. This novel, *The King David Report,* is apparently now to be published. The poet Reiner Kunze fell foul of the party because of his ties with Czech literary circles in 1968. Heym, and a number of other GDR writers, have managed to keep the wolf from the door by publishing in West Germany, without experiencing too much trouble from the East

wrong title

+ published in 60's, very amusing lampoon of Stalinist historical writing. 69

German authorities. Now, it seems, some of them will once again have the chance to influence the people they are really interested in, their fellow citizens of the GDR.

With films like Ulrich Plenzdorf's *Die Legende von Paul und Paula,* and possibly Lothar Warneke's *Leben mit Uwe,* DEFA is getting away from its strait-laced, over-optimistic view of the sex and married life of the GDR intelligentsia, and getting just a little nearer the more complex reality.[30]

Why, then, assuming that this really is the case, is there an easing up in the Democratic Republic's cultural life? There is no obvious answer, but there are one or two likely reasons. Though Honecker was never regarded as a friend of the writers in Ulbricht's time, it may be that, now he is safely on the throne, he feels he can afford to be less cautious and more tolerant. His wife, Margot Honecker, Minister of Education, could be an influence in this more 'liberal' direction. In addition, Honecker may feel it necessary to win the sympathy of writers in order to meet the challenge of *Ostpolitik* more successfully. If they — some of whom have been applauded in the West, and some of whom are perhaps better known in the GDR due to the interest shown in them by the Western media — could be lined up four-square behind the party, they would have a stabilising effect. This is a good time to seek an alliance with them, because they are united both in their condemnation of the military junta in Chile and their approval of the changes in Portugal and Greece, and because inflation and crisis have made the West look less appetising than it did. The 'liberal' tactic will not only improve the GDR's image both at home and abroad: it will also disarm potential rebels and make it easier to get certain vital theses accepted. These are: (i) that, instead of there being one German culture, there are two separate mutually antagonistic, socialist and capitalist German cultures; (ii) that the example of Chile shows that armed vigilance is necessary and can be achieved only through close ties with the USSR; and (iii) that it therefore is necessary to uproot any attempt to weaken the USSR (for instance, through the means used by Solzhenitsyn) or the GDR's links with the Soviets (through bourgeois nationalism). Though Solzhenitsyn was not mentioned, these were the political theses accepted by the Seventh Writers' Congress of the GDR in November 1973.[31]

Clearly, the eagerness shown by the Soviet leaders to court Herr Brandt, and the assurances of continuing *détente* that they have given his successor, Helmut Schmidt, must have raised fears in the minds of the members of the SED's Politburo. Though, logically and rationally, they do not take such an eventuality seriously, the possibility that the Soviets could do a deal with West Germany that would eventually lead to the liquidation of their state must surely nag at them. Such a sell-out is unlikely. In military terms, the GDR stands second only to the USSR in the Warsaw pact. [32] In economic and technological terms, it is a significant factor in the Soviet economy. [33] Above all, in ideological terms, such a deal would rob the USSR of its leading role as protector of revolutionary powers, and would undermine its whole position in Eastern Europe. The main danger to the GDR from East-West détente comes not from such deals, but from the infectious ideas of West Germans visiting the Republic. It comes also from the SED's inability, out of deference to the Soviet Union and the changing situation, to make the same strident attacks on West Germany as it did until 1969. For instance, the East German press was careful not to attack Willy Brandt when he was Chancellor, though attacks were made on some of his colleagues, including Helmut Schmidt. The changes that have come about are indicated by the case of Herbert Wehner, Chairman of the SPD. Wehner, probably the most significant individual in German social democracy since the war, was long under attack as a 'renegade'. However, after June 1973, when he was received by Erich Honecker at the latter's country home, such attacks became impossible. In other words, despite continued attacks on West German capitalism, the alleged persecution of Communists in West Germany, and so on, *Ostpolitik* has forced the SED to tone down its attacks on the Federal Republic, especially on members of the ruling SPD/FDP élite. Thus it becomes more difficult for it to expect and insist that its own people retain the old, extreme *Feindbild* (picture of the enemy). This in turn makes ordinary East Germans more receptive to Western ideas.

But how are average East Germans reacting to their Western visitors? Is there a growing alienation between the East Germans and the West Germans? Undoubtedly the differences have grown. Just as the Briton who has lived in Canada or Australia for ten or twenty years finds he is no longer quite at home in 'the old country', and no longer quite at one with his former compatriots, so too the West German visitor finds he is no longer quite at home in Dresden, Halle or Magdeburg. Apart from that, more and more citizens of the two German states have known only the régimes they now live under. The older generation with a political past in common is gradually giving way to a new generation who do not share this background. By 1971, over 10 million East Germans out of a population of 17 millions were less than forty-one years old. This means that they were under fifteen in 1945, and that their appreciation of politics is therefore restricted to the People's Democracy model. About another 2·5 million were under seventeen in 1933, and have thus known only Nazism and Communism. Yet many of these have relatives, even brothers and sisters in the West, and they watch Western television — though this rarely involves a conscious political act. It is amazing how far 'bourgeois' values remain, even among those schooled exclusively in the GDR. Arthur M. Hanhardt found evidence of this among East German youth in the 1960s. [34] He also found a widespread lack of political conviction among these young people, who tended not to have any deep pro- or anti-GDR feelings.

Just as it would be unwise to underestimate alienation as a factor in relations between East and West Germans, so it would be foolish to overemphasise it. In addition to their family ties and common heritage, the citizens of the two countries could find a lot to talk to each other about: TV programmes and their influence; sex, marriage, and birth control; women's place in society; education and their children's future; the gulf between youth and the older generation; military service, its usefulness or otherwise; modern housing and the environment.

In conclusion, the widespread international recognition of the GDR, due in part to the *Ostpolitik,* must make the East German régime more acceptable to its own people. The state's fantastic sporting achievements must help to swell the pride of its citizens. The knowledge of its growing economic strength, and reports from Western television about the West's economic and social ills, will help in the stabilisation process, as will the improvements in living standards. Yet, in a way, these improvements remove a barrier between the citizens of the two Germanies (who in any case still have much in common). In the old days, East Germans got tired of being patronised by West Germans, from Adenauer downwards. Talk about *'die armen Brüder und Schwestern in der Zone'* ('the poor brothers and sisters in the Soviet Zone') ceased to be appreciated, particularly as no 'liberation' came. With decent living standards comparable to those across the frontier, the East Germans will be less on the defensive, and serious discussion between the two Germanies will become likely, with possible influences on them both. Thus, the human contacts initiated by the *Ostpolitik* could be beneficial to both East and West.

Unfortunately, however, the GDR cannot be deemed fully sovereign and independent. Its future, even its internal political, economic and social arrangements, is still decisively influenced by the Soviet Union. Though it does not face many of the same problems as the USSR (the Jews, for example), it is influenced by them. In this situation, any attempt to assess its future stability is of limited value if it does not try simultaneously to assess the future development of the Soviet state and Soviet society.

Notes

[1] For the early period in the Soviet Zone GDR, see the serious account by J.P. Nettl (*The Eastern Sone and Soviet Policy in Germany, 1945–50*, London 1951), and the impressionistic one by W.G.J. Knop (*Prowling Russia's Forbidden Zone. A Secret Journey into Soviet Germany*, New York 1949), see also W. Leonhard, *Die Revolution Entlässt Ihre Kinder*, Cologne 1955.

[2] For the economy up to the early 1960s, see Nettl, op. cit., W.F. Stolper, *The Structure of the East German Economy*, Cambridge, Mass., 1960, A. Zauberman, *Industrial Progress in Poland, Czechoslovakia and East Germany, 1937–62*, London 1964; and K.C. Thalheim, *Die Wirtschaft der Sowjetzone in Krise und Umbau*, West Berlin 1964.

[3] E. Richert, *Sozialistische Universität. Die Hochschulpolitik der SED*, West Berlin 1967.

[4] On East German propaganda, see E. Richert, *Agitation und Propaganda: Das System der publizistischen Massenführung in der Sowjetzone*, West Berlin 1958; and H. Köhler, *Zur geistigen und seelischen Situation der Menschen in der Sowjetzone*, Bonn 1954.

[5] A. Baring, *Der 17. Juni 1953*, Cologne 1966; H. Brandt, *Ein Traum, der nicht entführbar ist. Mein Weg zwischen Ost und West*, Munich 1967; S. Brant, *Der Aufstand*, Stuttgart 1954; *Der Volksaufstand vom 17. Juni 1953;* Ministry for All-German Affairs, Bonn 1968.

[6] Among the books covering the GDR in the 1960s are H. Apel, *DDR, 1962, 1964, 1966*, West Berlin 1967; David Childs, *East Germany*, London 1969; Marion Gräfin Dönhoff, R.W. Leonhardt and T. Sommer, *Reise in ein fernes Land*, Hamburg 1964; Welles Hangen, *The Muted Revolution*, London 1967; Arthur M. Hanhardt, *The German Democratic Republic*, Baltimore 1968; Joachim Nawrocki, *Das geplante Wunder*, Hamburg 1967; Wolfgang Plat, *Begegnung mit den anderen Deutschen*, Hamburg 1969; Jean Edward Smith, *Germany Beyond the Wall*, Boston 1968; and Hermann Weber, *Von der SBZ zur DDR 1945–68*, Hanover 1968.

[7] It is of course difficult to know just how far this thaw was influenced by internal considerations, and how much by events in the Soviet Union.

[8] See Chancellor Kiesinger's reference to them in his speech of 11 March 1968.

[9] Apel, op.cit.

[10] On Ulbricht, see Carola Stern, *Ulbricht: a Political Biography*, New York, 1965; F. Schenk, *Im Vorzimmer der Diktatur*, Cologne 1962; and E.W. Gniffke, *Jahre mit Ulbricht*, Cologne 1966.

[11] Peter C. Ludz, *Parteielite im Wandel*, Cologne 1970, and *The German Democratic Republic from the Sixties to the Seventies*, Cambridge, Mass., 1970.

[12] *Die Zeit*, 12 October 1973, p.2.

[13] 'Bericht über die Lage der Nation' in *Das Parlament*, 2 February 1974, p.2.

[14] Albert Norden in *Der Morgen*, 26 January 1974.

[15] Günter Mittag in *Der Morgen*, 8 December 1972.

[16] Kurt Hager in *Der Morgen*, 29 December 1973. See also *Einheit* no. 2, 1974, for the SED's current view of social democracy.

[17] *Der Morgen*, 20 June 1974.

[18] *Der Morgen*, 8 December 1972. This servile attitude to the Soviet Union is indicated by the fact that the rulers of the GDR seem to believe that no East German is capable of producing a monument worthy of Lenin. The main Lenin monument in the GDR is in Berlin, and was conceived by the Soviet artist Nikolai Tomski. Another important one, due to be unveiled in Dresden in 1974, is the work of another Soviet artist, Professor Jastrebenezki of Leningrad (see *Der Morgen*, 15 November 1973).

[19] *Die Zeit*, 1 March 1974.

[20] *Der Morgen*, 3 November 1973.

[21] *Vörwarts* (Bonn) 14 February 1974.

[22] *Die Wirtschaft*, 1 August 1974; see *Einheit* no. 4, 1974, for a discussion of housing problems.

[23] *Der Morgen*, 18 January 1974.

[24] All these figures are given in the *Statistical Pocket Book of the German Democratic Republic, 1972*, Staatsverlag der DDR, 1972, pp. 56–8. For the 1961 percentages see Childs, *East Germany*, op.cit., p.163.

[25] *Der Morgen*, 1 May 1974.

[26] See Martin Schnitzer, *East and West Germany: a Comparative Economic Analysis*, New York, 1972, p. 38.

[27] *Democratic German Report*, 17 May 1972.

[28] *Statistical Pocket Book, 1972*, pp.19 and 30.

[29] W.L. Webb, 'The wind in the East' in *The Guardian*, 6 April 1974. See also Webb's earlier articles in *The Guardian* (issues of 10 and 12 April 1973).

[30] For a discussion of the film *Die Legende von Paul und Paula*, see *Die Zeit Magazin*, 29 March 1974. The film was also discussed, in relation to more general tendencies on the cultural front, in *Die Zeit*, 20 April 1974.

[31] The declaration of the Writers' Congress was given in the East German press on 17 November 1973. For Western appreciations of the

congress see, among others, *Die Zeit,* 23 November 1973, and *Vȯrwarts,* 22 November 1973.

[32] See Dale Roy Herspring, *East German Civil-Military Relations. The Impact of Technology 1949–72,* New York 1973, p.152.

[33] See Schnitzer, op. cit. See also Eberhard and Hans Dieter Schulz's authoritative *Braucht der Osten die DDR?,* Opladen 1968.

[34] Arthur M. Hanhardt, Jr., *Political Socialization in the German Democratic Republic,* paper prepared for delivery at the sixty-sixth Annual Meeting of the American Political Science Association, September 1970.

4 The Ostpolitik and Relations Between the Two Germanies

Geoffrey K. Roberts

> We know that many — I would rather say, the majority — of the citizens of the GDR see our policy, which culminated in the treaties with Moscow and Warsaw and the agreements with East Berlin, as a hope, a hope that things in Germany will improve, that once again we can draw near one another and that thus the idea of the German nation is not, and need not be, abandoned.
>
> Willy Brandt, addressing the Bundestag on 10 May 1972[1]

The background to the German question

The unification of Germany under Bismarck was one solution to the 'German question', that problem of national identity that has plagued the German people — and their neighbours — for so long. That it was not a permanent solution was due, to a large extent, to the lack of congruence between the economic and the political development of the German state, and to the social consequences of this.[2] After the First World War, Bavarian and Rhenish particularism and the territorial adjustments made by the peace treaties kept the national question open. The immoderate expansion of Germany under the Third Reich, and its inevitable consequence, the Second World War, aggravated the situation: it was impossible to equate the greatly extended boundaries of the German Empire with an acceptable permanent solution to the problem of what constituted Germany. However, it was by no means obvious that the settlement after the war, however it might be arrived at, would involve anything as drastic as the development of two separate and independent German states, with very different and mutually antagonistic social and economic orders; nor that they would become important members of opposed military alliances, and strong units in different multinational trading organisations.

Of course, as the war entered its closing stages, the Allies gave consideration to the question of the future of a defeated Germany. The Morgenthau Plan for the deindustrialisation of Germany was one strategy proposed. Others included various forms of dismemberment and division, such as those discussed at the Teheran Conference in 1943. Once the war had ended, however, plans for zones of occupation were put into effect, and the Potsdam Conference in 1945 assumed that Germany would some day be reunited, and that in the meantime the four zones should nevertheless form a single economic unit.

However, the geographical locations of the zones of occupation (with the Russian Zone adjacent to other Russian-controlled territory), and the growing mistrust between the Soviet Union and the Western Allies, combined to make it more and more difficult to treat Germany as a unit in any way whatsoever. Consequently, the division between East and West became more and more marked. Prior to 1949, West Germany had this choice: to opt for independent status, though with certain restrictions on her sovereignty, or to keep open the possibility of reunification under terms that would include some type of neutralisation, and thus the danger of later Russian domination. It could not hope for both reunification and independence. For East Germany, even this choice was not available, and it became ever more securely meshed in the Russian-dominated Communist bloc.

Given the geo-political situation in 1949, the choice of independent status rather than reunification was plainly the obvious one, and the foreign policy pursued by Adenauer in the first few years of his Chancellorship was only the logical fulfilment of this choice. Russia had occupied Eastern Europe, and she controlled the territories she occupied by turning them into Communist states. East Germany, though also an 'independent state' once the Federal Republic came into being in 1949, was one of the most closely controlled units of Stalin's empire, and its economy was milked by Russia in the name of reparations. Clearly, the Federal Republic felt endangered by the proximity of Russian troops and the expansionist aims of the Soviet government. In this situation, Adenauer sought the protection of the United States (later through membership of NATO), and hence his policy of close identification with the West was a logical necessity. His policy towards East Germany was a consequence of his foreign policy in general, and thus tended to be passive, reacting to events rather than initiating moves towards better relations. Proposals for a solution involving reunification were made from time to time, often involving neutralisation, but none of these options were realistic in the circumstances. The Berlin rising of 1953 (the anniversary of which — on 17 June — is now celebrated in the Federal

Republic as the 'Day of German Unity') served only to demonstrate the sterility of any policy based on internal revolt in the German Democratic Republic.

The division between the two Germanies became still more permanent when, in 1955, the Federal Republic joined NATO, and the GDR the Warsaw Pact alliance. The claims of the Federal Republic to represent all the German people, on the grounds that those in the 'Soviet Zone of Occupation' (the official appellation of the GDR in the Federal Republic) could not exercise freedom of political choice, and the Hallstein Doctrine, by which the Federal Republic made it known that it would not entertain diplomatic relations with any third country (other than the Soviet Union) that recognised the GDR, also increased the gap between the two states. East Germany continued to believe in reunification – on its own terms. The refugee groups and Right-wing political parties in West Germany maintained an uncompromising attitude towards the question of reunification, an attitude that was only hardened when the Berlin wall was erected in 1961. This wall, which divided Berlin itself, almost totally dried up the flow of refugees to the West, and symbolised in very material terms the division of Germany – and also the division of Europe.

The erection of the Berlin Wall may also be taken to mark the nadir of inter-German relations since the war. Towards the end of the Adenauer era, several changes became visible, offering the possibility of a new orientation for the Federal Republic's Eastern policy in general, and for its policy towards relations with East Germany in particular. First, there were changes in the international context: the Cold War was being translated into a balance of deterrents situation, within which some degree of contact and accommodation between East and West was becoming possible. Secondly, a new generation, unconcerned and unconnected with the Nazi past, but very much concerned with the politics of the present, was making its presence felt in the Federal Republic; the basically Left-wing sympathies of these people left them at least willing to explore the possibility of better relations with East Germany. Thirdly, East Germany itself was becoming consolidated, finding a new prosperity and a new self-confidence behind the Wall, which had stopped the emigration of its skilled work-force, its intelligentsia, and its professional specialists.

These changes became apparent in the closing years of Adenauer's, and during Erhard's, Chancellorship, but it was during the years of the Grand Coalition, when Kiesinger was Chancellor and Brandt Foreign Minister, that the most definite signs of a change towards East Germany appeared. Despite the Hallstein Doctrine, diplomatic relations were established with Yugoslavia and Romania. Kiesinger also tried to begin negotiations with

East Germany on a number of concrete issues, such as increased economic co-operation, and scientific, technical and cultural exchange agreements, but these proposals were ignored by the East German authorities, who instead proposed negotiations over the 'normalisation of relations'. This, to the East Germans, would have implied full diplomatic recognition, viewed as anathema by successive West German governments, and unthinkable even to one composed of the two major parties. Indeed, Kiesinger's government declaration following his accession to the Chancellorship had stressed the continuance of the Federal Republic's claim to be the 'sole representative' of the German people as a whole, and the fact that his government could not consider recognition of the GDR as a foreign state, much as he wished for closer relations.

In April 1969, the Free Democratic Party, who were among the first to change fundamentally their position on the issue in the name of realism, put down a major question on it to the government. This led to the airing of the whole issue in the Bundestag, and the government indicated that it would 'not exclude' the possibility of a treaty with East Germany to 'regulate relations', at least until a proper peace treaty, dealing with the position of both Germanies, could be concluded. However, the attitude of the East German government remained unchanged. In a press statement replying to Kiesinger's earliest approaches, Hermann, the East German Secretary for West German Questions, emphasised the anti-GDR interpretations that could be placed on the statements, activities and existing treaty obligations of the Federal Republic, and accused the 'Kiesinger–Strauss' government of revanchist motives. He further stressed that peaceful relations between the two Germanies were impossible without the full diplomatic recognition of the GDR by the Federal Republic.

As the West German general election of 1969 approached – and with it the likelihood that the Right-wing extremist National Democratic Party, an implacable opponent of negotiations with the GDR, would enter the Bundestag – 'the question was whether the German people could measure up to the greatest burden that could be imposed upon a nation – namely, that of remaining a nation once the protective skin of a unified state had been broken'.[3]

Breaking the ice

'By the end of the Grand Coalition, relations between the two German states had reached an impasse.'[4] It seemed that the Federal Republic

80

could not change the situation without according the GDR diplomatic recognition, yet this still seemed to be too high a price for any West German government to pay. However, it seems clear that Kiesinger underestimated the extent to which public opinion on East Germany was changing: poll results in fact suggested that a large majority of the population favoured direct talks with the East Germans, and that there was even a majority in favour of formal recognition. The result of the 1969 election allowed the Social Democrats to form a coalition with the Free Democrats, and made the Christian Democrats an opposition party for the first time; there was now an opportunity for a completely new approach to the problem of relations between the two Germanies. This new approach was soon forthcoming: Brandt's government declaration indicated his willingness to seek better and closer relations with East Germany, as well as with Russia and other Eastern bloc countries. His Foreign Minister, Walter Scheel, and his special negotiator, Egon Bahr, commenced soundings in preparation for a programme of treaties that would normalise relations, and bring a sense of realism and security to West Germany's dealings with her Eastern neighbours. Meanwhile, the GDR had been quietly developing a more independent foreign policy, less linked to Russian requirements, and was becoming increasingly successful in its search for diplomatic recognition by non-Communist countries. Its government was also very conscious of the benefits of trade with the Federal Republic, and to this extent there was a readiness, but a confident readiness, to consider proposals from the Federal Republic for better relations.[5]

This willingness on the part of both German governments to explore the possibilities of negotiation led to two meetings between Willy Brandt and Willi Stoph, Prime Minister of East Germany. The first of these meetings took place on 19 March 1970 at Erfurt, in East Germany, after the GDR had first tried to have East Berlin accepted as the location. The opening speeches set out the positions of the two governments, and nothing definite was mentioned in the closing communiqué other than agreement to a second meetings, this time at Kassel, in West Germany. One factor that seemed to cause much concern to the East German authorities was the extravagant welcome that the crowd gave Brandt. A few days after the Erfurt meeting, Stoph made a speech to the East German parliament stressing that the aim of his government was peace, and hence that it sought nothing less than full diplomatic recognition from the Federal Republic.

The meeting at Kassel on 21 May 1970 made little or no advance on the positions stated at Erfurt. Brandt put forward twenty points for discussion and negotiation between the two governments, but Stoph reiterated the demands of his government for full diplomatic recognition and the accession of both German states to the United Nations. Brandt's thesis that the 'unity of the nation' depended more on a 'feeling of belonging together', which existed and should be developed, than on being members of a single state and social order found no response from the East Germans. The hostile reception given to Stoph by members of Right-wing extremist groups, including the destruction of the East German flag flying in front of the place where Stoph and Brandt were meeting, provided Stoph with grounds for charges that the Federal Republic still harboured 'revanchist' ideals. Despite the symbolic significance of these first meetings between government leaders from the two German states, the results in concrete terms seemed negligible. The East German element of the new *Ostpolitik* appeared to have failed almost before it had got under way.

However, a number of things were happening that were to have an influence on relations between East and West Germany. Negotiations with the Russian and Polish governments were brought to a successful conclusion later in 1970, with the signing of the Moscow and Warsaw treaties. In the Moscow Treaty, the validity of the East German border with West Germany was formally accepted by the Federal Republic, in itself a kind of substitute 'diplomatic recognition'. The consequences of this treaty were of great significance for relations between the two Germanies. For West Germany, it was a stimulus towards the acceptance of political reality, since it could then be said that 'the limited success of the *Ostpolitik* has been diluted by the continuing failure of Bonn's *Deutschlandpolitik*', making it necessary to make progress with the GDR. For East Germany, it meant pressure from Moscow to adopt a more flexible position towards West German demands. The signing of the Moscow Treaty did, in any case, act as a shock to the East Germans' view of East–West relations, since it 'violated the key axiom of East German policy ... that no move towards normalisation of relations with the Federal Republic would be made without reciprocal concessions by Bonn towards recognition of East Berlin'. The signing of the Four-Power Agreement on Berlin in September 1971 − again to the benefit of West Germany and resulting in further pressure being placed on East Germany by the Russians − was another momentous step. Thus it was not really surprising when, in November 1971, Egon Bahr and State Secretary Kohl of the GDR began a long series of talks that, in the course of two years, were to involve some seventy meetings.

The first fruits of these talks were agreements covering transit traffic between West Germany and West Berlin, and tourist and commercial traffic. These agreements were partly the result of the Four-Power Agreement on Berlin, and were concluded in December 1971 and May 1972. They were important not only for their intrinsic effects, but also for their influence on the development of political relations between the Federal Republic and the GDR. In May 1972, the parties represented in the Bundestag issued a joint declaration approving of 'normalisation of relations' between the two Germanies: This was another encouraging sign, and helped to open up the way for a general treaty formalising such 'normalisation', and make it possible for further progress to be made on other questions of concern to the Federal Republic and the GDR.

The Basic Treaty

The 'Treaty on the Basis of Relations between the Federal Republic of Germany and the German Democratic Republic' — referred to by Brandt as 'the instrument for organising co-operation under the prevailing circumstances'[6] was initialled in Bonn on 8 November 1972 by the two men, Bahr and Kohl, whose patient negotiation had made it possible. The main clauses provided that

- the two German republics should develop normal relations with each other on the basis of equal rights (Article 1);
- disputes between the two states should be settled by peaceful means and not by the threat or use of force, the frontiers between the two states being inviolable, and each state under an obligation to respect the other's territorial integrity (Article 3);
- neither state could represent the other internationally (Article 4);
- both republics should proceed on the principle that the sovereign jurisdiction of each state is confined to its own territory (Article 6);
- co-operation should be developed in such fields as science, transport, judicial relations, and sport, the details being regulated by supplementary protocols (Article 7);
- permanent missions would be exchanged (Article 8);
- existing treaty obligations would not be affected by the Basic Treaty (Article 9).

While these provisions were open to varying interpretations, many aspects of the treaty were of importance for both states. It is significant that the treaty left many crucial questions 'in the air', especially the Federal Republic's claim to represent West Berlin, and its insistence that there was some form of 'special relationship' between the two Germanies, preventing either from being 'foreign' to the other.[7] What the treaty did do, however, was to formalise the Federal Republic's recognition of the GDR as a state, and greatly reduce its claim (under the Basic Law) to be the sole representative of all Germans; this had been diminished, if not totally invalidated, by Article 4 of the treaty. For East Germany, the treaty meant recognition of its international status as a separate and independent state, but at the cost of concessions on such matters as increased East-West contacts — which could affect, even endanger, its internal political and ideological stability. For West Germany, it meant a painful recognition of reality, though the preservation of its relationship with West Berlin, and the improvement of access to what its government regarded as the 'other part' of the German nation, could be counted as benefits.

Equally important were the supplementary protocols, which enlarged on the bald statements of the treaty itself and marked agreement on definite steps towards the implementation of the 'co-operation' envisaged in Article 7. A commission would be set up to review and define the existing frontier between the two states. Trade would be developed 'on the basis of existing agreements'. This was of great importance to East Germany, for the Federal Republic is its largest trading partner after the Soviet Union, and this relationship provides advantages in terms of access to other countries of the European Economic Community, interest-free deficits on trading balances, and so forth; certainly, in this field the GDR seems only too happy to accept the existence of a 'special relationship'. Existing agreements in the field of traffic and telecommunications were to be extended, building on the treaty of May 1972 in the first case, and on agreements reached in 1970 and 1971 in the second. Promises were also exchanged to enter into negotiations on questions of co-operation in the areas of judicial relations, health, culture, sport, and environmental protection; and discussions about the exchange of publications and radio and television programmes were envisaged. Supplementary exchanges of correspondence promised improvements in matters affecting divided families; in the status and privileges of West German journalists working in the GDR, and *vice-versa* and in access from one state to the other, by the provision of additional border crossing-points. Finally, both governments agreed to make simultaneous application for membership of the United Nations. In March 1974, after considerable delay and bargaining, a protocol agreeing details of the exchange of permanent representatives was signed by representatives of the two states. It was agreed that GDR's representative in West Germany would be accredited to the Chancellery in

Bonn, and the Federal Republic's in the GDR to the Foreign Office in East Berlin. The avoidance of the title 'embassy' for these diplomatic missions was, of course, a victory for the West German claim that neither state is 'foreign' to the other.

The 'objective' effects of the treaty lie mainly in the future, though increased West German tourist traffic to the GDR, membership of the United Nations, and the exchange of permanent representatives are very real and positive indications that 'fings ain't what they used to be' in the days of Adenauer and Ulbricht. In particular, 'for the GDR, entry into the United Nations is the crowning of its diplomatic breakthrough'.[8] The gains sought by the Federal Republic in terms of increased contact with the GDR have materialised only slowly and in part, and will depend on applying constant pressure to a sometimes very obstructive and reluctant East German government. But the 'objective' effects are not the whole story; nor is it to be thought that either government supposed that they would be. Also of importance are the 'subjective' effects, the effects the new relationship might have on the political situation in both countries.

The West German perspective

'The treaty does not solve the German question; rather it leaves it more open than before.'[9]

The effects of the process of normalisation on attitudes within the Federal Republic were diverse, ranging from outright hostility and charges of betrayal from Right-wing nationalists, to gratitude and expressions of hope from those with most to gain from improved access to East Germany.

Because of these divergent attitudes towards the treaty, and the different positions taken by the parties of the governing coalition on the one hand and the opposition on the other, one might have thought that the country was as divided as the Bundestag seemed to be. [10] The long period during which there was a taboo on political discussion of any move to recognise East Germany as an independent state had, however, tended to disguise the decline in public concern about reunification. In the past, especially in times of economic well-being, [11] reunification had been a salient issue for the public; but the aging of the population had diluted the political strength of the refugee groups that had done so much to keep the matter alive. In accepting the SPD/FDP alliance in 1969, the electorate had given a mandate for a more realistic, up-to-date approach to the question of inter-German relations. This was no sudden conversion. A new generation, with new political orientations, had reached voting age; and, despite the difficulties of obtaining information about 'over there', their picture of East Germany was not so coloured by post-war fears of Communist expansion as to prevent acceptance of the reality that the GDR was a state independent of the Federal Republic.

It was to Brandt's advantage that he had been sensitive to these changing attitudes even before he became Chancellor. His experience as Foreign Minister in the Grand Coalition, his ties with West Berlin as a former Mayor of the city, his contacts with FDP members anxious to obtain a relaxation of the rigid official policy towards East Germany, all made him conscious of the opportunity for a new approach to the German question, an approach based on realism rather than dogma. His government declaration in 1969 was a first demonstration of his readiness for negotiation with East Berlin, and his attitude, and that of his government, was repeatedly expressed in Bundestag debates, in party statements, in press conferences, and in official publications. Brandt's thesis was that there still existed a single German nation, but that this nation was at present divided into two quite independent states, a division that was unlikely to be ended in the foreseeable future. [12] Anything that would maintain the sense of national unity among Germans should be done, short of according the GDR official recognition as a 'foreign' state. Certainly, negotiation, recognition of the borders between the two German states, and acceptance of the independent status of the GDR were no longer excluded as means of fostering this national unity, especially if concessions could be obtained that would improve contact and communication between East and West Germans. The whole of the *Ostpolitik* may be seen as contributing to this improvement of relations with the GDR; indeed, the conclusion of the Basic Treaty had been judged by one commentator to be the most weighty short-term goal of the *Ostpolitik*. [13] Of course, not all that was desirable could be obtained; in particular, the freedom of East German citizens to visit the West was little improved. But Brandt emphasised that it was better to open a few one-way streets than to reject the whole enterprise. [14] Indeed, the result of the negotiations not only safeguarded the Federal Republic's position with regard to Berlin, but also left open the option of peacefully pursuing the goal of reunification. In this and other ways, the treaty could be seen as making it possible to develop links with East Germany that went well beyond the substantive areas mentioned in the protocols.

The Free Democrats, proud of the initiatives that they had taken on inter-German relations as long ago as 1958, supported the steps taken by the Brandt-Scheel coalition and were able to demonstrate that these steps had almost completely fulfilled the demands they had made in their 1969 election campaign.

For the opposition parties – the Christian Democrats and the Christian Socialists – the situation was more complex. On the one hand, they could not deny Brandt's success (honoured by the Nobel Peace Prize and other signs of international acclaim), and there were strong feelings within these parties that to oppose the gains that the government had made would be mistaken, both morally and electorally. On the other hand, uncritical acceptance of Brandt's *Deutschlandpolitik* would be opposed by many influential sections of the CDU/CSU, and would seem to be delivering a major political advantage to the ruling coalition. Neither Kiesinger nor Barzel, as leaders of the opposition after 1969, succeeded in resolving this dilemma. The Bundestag debates on the Basic Treaty in January 1974 showed that the opposition attitude was little changed, despite the fact that it had suffered defeat in the 1972 election, and that this had led to the resignation of Barzel from the leadership. Opposition speakers such as Carstens, the leader of the parliamentary opposition group, suggested that the *Ostpolitik* had given the Communist countries everything they had asked for, but that none of the goals of the Federal Republic – unity of the nation, the advancement of human rights in Communist states, and the closer linking of West Berlin to the Federal Republic – had been secured. The Bavarian government's unsuccessful attempt to challenge the treaty on the grounds of its incompatibility with the Basic Law, in the Federal Constitutional Court, may also be regarded as symptomatic of the opposition's attitude. However consistent this attitude may have been in terms of the past – particularly in view of Adenauer's vigorous anti-Communist and pro-Western foreign policies – it is unlikely to have been of much electoral advantage to the CDU/CSU, for even the business interests who most strongly support them see potential advantages in closer relations with the GDR.

For West Germany as a whole, then, the prospect after the signing of the Basic Treaty is, on balance, favourable. The fundamental issue of relations with the GDR seems to have been settled, though the opposition may be expected to remain sensitive to any signs that the East Germans are going back on their side of the bargain – by raising the minimum amounts of currency that have to be exchanged on travelling to the East, by restricting access or obstructing transit traffic, or by imposing new restrictions on their own citizens – while, for all parties, the periodic wounding and killing of would-be refugees on the border will continue to be a matter for concern and for protest. A quarter of a century after unconditional surrender, the West Germans can more easily try to come to terms with the fact of a divided nation. In terms of security, it can be argued that the *Ostpolitik* as a whole has been disadvantageous to the Western Alliance, upon which the security of the Federal Republic against Russian invasion ultimately depends;[15] equally, the Basic Treaty, like the Moscow Treaty, may be regarded as removing certain very dangerous excuses for the type of border incident, in Germany or in Berlin, that could spark off a major conflagration. The increase in number of tourists visiting East Germany, slight but perceptible improvements in the transfer of publications and in cultural contacts, even the increase in sporting contacts (exemplified by the famous match between the two German teams in the 1974 World Cup) all provide grounds for hope that the process of 'drawing nearer' may in fact be under way. Not that the picture lacks its shading: the 'Guillaume case', in which an East German spy was discovered in Chancellor Brandt's entourage early in 1974, and the subsequent resignation of Brandt, supplied an unpleasant corrective to over-rosy images of a new mood of friendly co-operation between Bonn and East Berlin . Not surprisingly, in view of the circumstances of his accession to the Chancellorship, Helmut Schmidt, Brandt's successor, has appeared much less ready to make any further advances to East Germany without very real reciprocal advantages being obtained for the Federal Republic.

The East German perspective

'Today one can no longer speak of a single German nation.'[16]

The process of adjusting from a confrontation situation to one of at least limited co-operation has been just as difficult in the German Democratic Republic as in the Federal Republic. Despite the GDR's attainment of its prime goals — diplomatic recognition, and entry into the UN — the Basic Treaty and its consequences have presented the ruling élite with a grave challenge to their ideological and political predispositions.

One thing that was in any case undergoing change when negotiations began was the East Germans' views on reunification and the 'German nation'. Till 1969 at least, the official pronouncements of the government and the SED still referred to 'one German nation'.[17] The 1964 Treaty between Russia and the GDR mentioned reunification as something to be obtained peacefully and democratically. This goal changed, for several reasons. For one thing, the 'legitimacy deficit'[18] of the GDR as a state

88

seemed to require that emphasis be placed not on the *German* nationality of its citizens, but on their *East* German and Socialist characteristics. Thus, it might be said that the East Germans were developing a 'class concept' of nationhood, differentiating the Socialist and proletarian GDR from the capitalist and bourgeois Federal Republic. The later corollary of this, particularly evident during negotiations with the West German government, was the rejection of any idea of 'one German nation' or the existence of any kind of 'special relationship', which was seen as having no more reality than a similar relationship between West Germany and Austria. Yet the 'special relationship' was carefully fostered in questions of trade, and, more subtly, in the 'orientation function' — the standard of comparison, apparent in the way the example of the Federal Republic stimulated the GDR to innovate and modernise: 'The East German state must continually compare itself with the West German state — as it is more and more compared with it internationally.' [19]

The dilemma for the GDR's leadership is both clear and understandable. On the one hand, their desire for recognition, and pressure from the Russians, drew them towards an accommodation with West Germany. On the other hand, this accommodation threatened the isolation and policy of restricted contact with the West that had been regarded as vital to the development of a sense of identity. The fact that negotiations had to take place with a Social Democrat government made the situation more, rather than less, uncomfortable. The SED regarded the Social Democrats as a more dangerous enemy of the working class than the conservative CDU, a divider and misleader of the working class, and the change of government in 1969 was seen from East Berlin as a change of office-holders but not a change of 'power'. [20] The progress that this Social Democrat government made with Moscow was therefore all the more difficult for the East German government to come to terms with. How could it explain to its own citizens its intransigence, its refusal to negotiate, when the infallible Russian leadership had signed a treaty with the West Germans? How should East Germany react in foreign policy terms to what seemed so like a betrayal of the solidarity that it had come to regard as its right from the Russians? Bender, in his study of Brandt's *Ostpolitik*, makes an illuminating comparison between the shocked attitude of the East Germans and what the reaction of the West Germans would have been had Stoph negotiated a settlement directly with Washington or Paris. [21] Ultimately, the demands that the West Germans made for progress towards closer ties with East Germany represented, for the GDR, a threat to its own security. Bonn's emphasis, as a reason for closer links, on the 'fact' that the citizens of the Federal Republic and the GDR were both

Germans was, for the East Germans, the very reason for avoiding such links. [22]

Once the Basic Treaty had been signed, the GDR authorities felt themselves bound to make it clear, to both East and West Germans, that nothing really had been conceded. Emphasis was placed on the diplomatic gains for the German Democratic Republic, and on its view that its relationship with the Federal Republic was in every way similar to its relationship with other capitalist states. East Germany would keep to 'the letter and the spirit' of the treaty, but — an obvious reference to West German opposition to that treaty — it had to be defended against its enemies.

Steps were taken within East Germany to check in advance some of the dangers that increased contacts with the West would bring once the treaty and its supplementary provisions had come into effect. Policemen, civil servants, soldiers, and others in 'sensitive' positions were 'encouraged' to avoid all types of contact with West Germans. One reason for this appears to have been the extent of public sympathy for Brandt and his policy towards the GDR revealed in East German opinion polls.[23] Progress on such matters as the exchange of permanent missions was slowed down for a while, though — again perhaps as a result of Moscow's concern about the threat to *détente* with the West — a softening of the GDR's attitude did become apparent later in 1974, and the permanent missions were set up as a result of an agreement signed on 14 March that year. The East Germans complained about the increased number of refugees smuggled to the west by commercial organisations, and blamed this on the traffic agreements; as a consequence, the West Germans were politically embarrassed. Another attempt at discouragement was the increase in the amount of East German currency that visitors to the GDR were obliged to purchase.

The GDR, like the Federal Republic, both gained and lost by the *Ostpolitik,* and by the Basic Treaty in particular. Whether the balance is favourable or otherwise will be revealed only over the longer term, and may well depend as much on the progress of East-West relations in general as on changes in the GDR's direct contacts with the Federal Republic.

The future of inter-German relations

'In the foreseeable future there can be no alternative but a Germany composed of two Germanies.' [24]

An examination of inter-German relations in the period during which the new *Ostpolitik* was developed demonstrates that on such a matter foreign and domestic politics become closely linked. However, it also shows neither German state can feasibly classify inter-German relations solely as domestic policy (since neither state has control over the other) or as foreign policy (since the common past and the special links of language, family, commerce, and so on, prevent this). Despite the protestations of the East German authorities, there *is* a special relationship, parallel in some ways to the relationship that, earlier in this century, linked Britons in the dominions to those at home. The problem is that West Germany wishes to foster, East Germany to dilute, that relationship. Time may be on the side of East Germany in this, but one authority has stressed that, to other people at least, both East and West Germans still feel compelled to register their sense of being 'German'. [25]

As regards the treaty itself, it would appear that it has removed some possible causes of tension, and has narrowed down the range of issues that could lead to conflict to two: reunification, and the status of West Berlin. This, however, may be an over-optimistic assessment: bitter experience and a wealth of lawyers have demonstrated that *'der Teufel steckt im Detail'* ('the Devil lurks among the details'), and it would not be at all surprising if the agreements signed by the two German governments were to lead to a endless succession of disputes and quarrels over such things as access for visitors, exit permission for East Germans in the 'cases of special need' anticipated by the agreements, post and telecommunications, joint action on environmental protection, and — matters that have so far been glossed over — the 'shooting order' and the smuggling of refugees.

Even supposing such problems did not arise, even supposing that normalisation led to further 'pragmatic' agreements permitting increased commercial, technological, cultural and familial contacts, the prospects for eventual reunification must be negligible. The fact that two German states have existed for a quarter of a century is the lesser obstacle; more significant is the divergence between those two states in terms of their cultural, political, and ideological development, and their symbolic significance for the alliance systems to which they belong. A 'convergence thesis' could perhaps be supported on the grounds that the two states' economies are to some extent complementary, and that the fact of their common past will continue to exert an attractive force; but for this convergence to go far, for it to proceed beyond, say, some more developed form of *modus vivendi* than exists at present, there would have to be a considerable convergence of East and West as a whole, or else a revival of some kind of neutralisation solution based on a peace settlement, resulting perhaps in the creation of a social-democratic German state that would separate Eastern from Western Europe. Such a solution would raise immense problems for the European Community and the economic integration of Eastern Europe, and could not occur without the GDR's resolving the dilemma posed by its desire for international status without the dangers of international contact. The resolution of this dilemma perhaps depends on a more confident relationship between rulers and ruled in the GDR, on more democracy and less authoritarian control. [26]

Ultimately, changes in relations between the two Germanies will continue to depend largely on the attitudes of other states, and especially the USA and the USSR. In their own interests, and in the interests of their smaller partners, they may continue to look askance at any process that seems likely to reunite the now enormous economic potentials of the two Germanies. The military danger is a lesser, but not a negligible, consideration. *Détente* and the removal of the tensions between the two states is one thing; agreement to a process of reunification is quite another.

The effects of improved relations on the internal political development of the two Germanies are impossible to forecast. Compared to inflation, the energy crisis, and changes in political attitudes, these effects may be of only minor significance. On the other hand, the negotiations *did* take place, hopes *were* raised, the treaty and supplementary agreements *have* been signed, and the domestic politics of neither country can remain unaffected. The *Ostpolitik* may not, in the end, prove to have done very much to improve relations between the GDR and the Federal Republic, but it has probably achieved the maximum that could realistically have been hoped for. [27]

Notes

[1] Quoted in Inner German Affairs, *Die Entwicklung der Beziehungen zwischen der Bundesrepublik Deutschland und der Deutschen Demokratischen Republik,* Bonn 1973, p.13.

[2] Ralf Dahrendorf, *Society and Democracy in Germany,* London 1968. See especially chapters 1–4, 26 and 27.

[3] Michael Freund, *From Cold War to Ostpolitik,* translated by R.W. Last, London 1972, p.58.

[4] L. Whetton, *Germany's Ostpolitik,* London 1971, p.33.

[5] Ibid., p.132.

[6] Press Conference, reported in the *Bulletin of the Federal Press and Information Office,* 9 November 1972.

[7] Wilhelm Kewenig, 'Die Bedeutung des Grundvertrags für das Verhältnis der beiden deutschen Staaten' in *Europa Archiv* vol. 28, no. 2, 1973, pp.42-5.

[8] Peter Christian Ludz, *Deutschlands doppelte Zukunft,* Munich 1974, p.173.

[9] 'Denkschrift' in Federal Press and Information Office, *Vertrag über die Grundlagen der Beziehungen zwischen der BRD und der DDR,* Bonn 1973, p.31.

[10] On the parties' attitudes to the *Ostpolitik* treaties generally, see Geoffrey K. Roberts, 'The West German Parties and the Ostpolitik' in *Government and Opposition,* vol. 7, no. 4, 1972.

[11] *Aussenpolitische Perspektiven des westdeutschen Staates,* vol. 2, Bonn 1972, p.59.

[12] 'Denkschrift', p.31.

[13] Kewenig, op.cit., p.37.

[14] Speech to the Bundestag on 24 January 1974, in *Das Parlament,* 2 February 1974.

[15] See, for example, R.H.C. Steed, 'Brandt's Eastern Mess of Pottage' in *The Daily Telegraph,* 18 July 1974.

[16] The SED's chief ideologist, Kurt Hager; quoted in *Der Spiegel* no. 52, 1972, p.41.

[17] *Aussenpolitische Perspektiven* . . . vol. 3 ('Der Zwang zur Partnerschaft'), pp.91-2.

[18] The concept is that of Professor Lepsius; cited in Ludz, op.cit., p.80.

[19] Ludz, op.cit., p.61.

[20] Peter Bender, *Die Ostpolitik Willy Brandts,* Hamburg 1972, p.90

[21] Ibid., p.91.

[22] Ibid., p.98.

[23] *Der Spiegel* no. 17, 1973, p.36.

[24] Freund, op.cit., p.121.

[25] Ludz, op.cit., p.100.

[26] *Aussenpolitische Perspektiven* . . . , vol.3 p.111.

[27] Bender, op.cit., p.99.

5 The Ostpolitik and West Germany's External Relations

Roger MORGAN

During the second half of the 1970s, the Federal Republic's attitude in international affairs will clearly be marked by a greater willingness to assert its national interests than the world was used to in the 1950s and 1960s. Bonn's readiness to stand up for these interests against the demands of its partners — illustrated at the end of 1973 by Brandt's refusal to accept the idea of a large EEC regional development fund, and in autumn 1974 by Schmidt's firm attitude on EEC agricultural prices — has at least four main causes.

First, the Federal Republic's massive economic strength inevitably increases its political bargaining power. With an economic output far greater than that of any of its EEC partners, West Germany — which pays in 30 per cent of the EEC budget and receives only 12 per cent of the payments from it — is in a powerful position in any negotiations with Britain, Italy or France. Even its particularly heavy dependence on imported oil has not proved a handicap to it, since its economic strength gives it the purchasing power to meet its needs.

Secondly, the inhibitions stemming from Germany's recent past are now much less powerful. The end of Hitler's Third Reich now lies almost a third of a century in the past, and the days when Chancellor Adenauer would make concessions to foreign governments in a spirit of contrition belong to the past as well. Willy Brandt's spectacular gesture of atonement in 1970, when he fell to his knees on the site of the Warsaw ghetto, was a moving plea that the past be forgiven; but the Germans of the 1970s are disinclined to let their political behaviour be dominated by the memory of these things. Most Germans alive today feel no personal responsibility for the misdeeds of the Third Reich, and this freedom from historical guilt is expressed in the policies of the government led by Chancellor Helmut Schmidt. The Federal Republic is no longer, as Willy Brandt described it when he was the opposition leader in 1965, 'an economic giant but a political dwarf': it is now psychologically ready to be a political giant too.

Thirdly, the Federal Republic's freedom of action, in the context of the

European Community, has been greatly enhanced by the way in which the Community itself has evolved into a much more loosely-structured organisation than its founders envisaged. Instead of the ever-increasing tightening-up of the integrative links, the impressive progression from economic to political union planned at the EEC's Paris summit conference of October 1972, the Community has, since 1973, been shaken by the crises of energy and inflation, as well as by the Italian imposition of import controls, French evasions of the agricultural policy, and the British Labour government's determination to renegotiate the terms of Britain's membership. This partial disintegration of the European Community has produced a German response in that Chancellor Schmidt, instead of preaching closer political union, as his predecessor did in 1973, attacks the bureaucracy for being inefficient and interfering, and argues that national governments should be still further emancipated from its trammels.

Fourthly, the *Ostpolitik* pursued by Chancellor Brandt between 1969 and 1973 has, by renouncing West Germany's claims for reunification with the GDR and the recovery of the Eastern territories, greatly increased her freedom of action *vis-à-vis* the West. This theme will be developed more fully below: the essential point is that the Federal Republic's refusal to recognise the GDR placed it to some extent at the mercy not only of African or Asian countries, which could bid one German state against the other as possible aid-donors, but also of the Western Allies, who could put pressure on Bonn by delicately hinting at an improvement of their own relations with the GDR. With Bonn's own recognition of East Berlin in 1973, these possibilities of leverage have been removed, and Bonn can afford to stand up more strongly to its Western partners. The effects of *Ostpolitik* on West Germany's international position have thus to be considered together with a number of other factors, all of which contribute to the increase of the Federal Republic's international power and freedom of action.

The actual substance of *Ostpolitik* is reflected in the package of treaties that resulted from the Brandt government's dynamic diplomacy from 1969 onwards. All these agreements had come into force by 1973. Chancellor Brandt and his adviser Egon Bahr, proceeding beyond the establishment of diplomatic relations with Yugoslavia and Romania in 1967, applied this renunciation of the Hallstein Doctrine to three more difficult 'targets' — Moscow, Warsaw and East Berlin. The complex negotiations between Bonn and these governments led first to treaties with the Soviet Union and Poland, which were worked out during Brandt's visits to Moscow and Warsaw in 1970, and then to a number of agreements between the two German states, of which the most important was the Basic Treaty (or *Grundvertrag*) signed late in 1972 and ratified in June 1973. (The delay in settling Bonn's differences with East Berlin was due partly to the deep-seated mutual mistrust of the two parties, and partly to the need for the Western Allies and the Soviet Union first to conclude the Berlin Agreement, which happened in September 1971.)

The text of these treaties and agreements, and the accompanying protocols and correspondence, runs into many pages, but their essential provisions are relatively simple. By the treaty with the Soviet Union — officially but misleadingly described as a 'Treaty on the Renunciation of Force' — the Federal Republic recognised the present frontier between East Germany and Poland (the Oder-Neisse Line) as Germany's permanent eastern frontier (at least pending the conclusion of a hypothetical treaty of peace between all the belligerents of the Second World War), and also undertook to negotiate a treaty setting up formal relations with the East German state. These twin components of the Moscow Treaty were in effect confirmed in Bonn's treaty with Warsaw. The Berlin Agreement — which was negotiated by the Western Allies and the Soviet Union, but which directly concerned relations between the two German states, and thus forms an integral part of Bonn's *Ostpolitik* — included among its main provisions the Soviet acceptance of close ties between West Berlin and West Germany, and of the right of West Berliners to visit East Berlin and the GDR (this had been impossible since 1961). In return, the Allies accepted the Soviet argument that West Berlin was not *part* of the Federal Republic. Finally, the Basic Treaty between the two German states provided for the establishment of formal official relations between them — even though the West German side, rejecting the idea that the second German state was a foreign country, refused to agree to full diplomatic relations as normally provided under international law.

All these treaties of a general political and legal nature were supplemented by technical agreements regulating traffic between the two German states and between West Berlin and West Germany. The end result of all this was the acceptance by all parties that there were now two German states, both of which duly took their seats in the United Nations in autumn 1973.

The first question to be asked about *Ostpolitik,* in relation to its significance for the external relations of the Federal Republic, is whether the policy carried through by Chancellor Brandt was static or dynamic in its effects. Outwardly, *Ostpolitik* had many static aspects. It represented a recognition of the territorial *status quo* bequeathed to Europe by the Second World War, including the division of the German nation into two states and the loss of the easternmost quarter of Germany's pre-war territory. The critics of Brandt's *Ostpolitik,* such as ex-Chancellor Kiesinger, emphasised this aspect of it when they called its supporters the *Anerkennungspartei* — the 'recognition party' — who were prepared to accept the hitherto unacceptable facts of Germany's post-war situation. (The same argument, incidentally, was applied by the same critics to the Brandt government's signature of the Non-Proliferation Treaty at the end of 1969 — an agreement that, in the words of Franz-Josef Strauss, signified for Germany 'an atomic Versailles of cosmic proportions'.)

However, this static element of *Ostpolitik* must be seen in perspective, since West Germany's readiness to accept the legal existence of the GDR in fact opened the way for a number of new developments in Bonn's foreign policy. In particular, the renunciation of West Germany's claim to be the only legitimate German state removed a number of inhibitions restricting her international freedom of movement.

The Federal Republic's foreign policy has, in fact, shown a marked degree of continuity ever since the state's foundation in 1949. This assertion may, of course, appear paradoxical, particularly as Adenauer's refusal to negotiate with the GDR throughout the 1950s is in distinct contrast to the development of inter-German relations in the 1970s; but the continuity lies in the fact that both Adenauer and Brandt saw the Federal Republic as *the* political unit, *the* actor in the international system, whose interests they were concerned to promote. Behind all Adenauer's rhetoric about the objective of German reunification — a goal that he appears at times to have taken seriously — lay the constant fact that reunification was for the time being impossible, if not actually undesirable from Adenauer's point of view. Consequently, the central policy concern was to further West Germany's international objectives — the prosperity, security, and political rehabilitation of the Federal Republic. Adenauer pursued these goals essentially in collaboration with Germany's Western allies, and thus without any thought of an active *Ostpolitik;* but throughout the negotiations of the 1950s — whether about the Coal and Steel Community, West German rearmament, or the Treaty of Rome — Adenauer acted as if the West German state, though legally a provisional entity, were in practical terms the organisation for whose interests he was working. His behaviour was reminiscent of the slogan promulgated by Eduard Bernstein at the turn of the century, in the debates on revisionism in the German Social Democratic Party: 'the end result means nothing to me, the movement means everything'. German reunification had the same significance for Adenauer as the Socialist revolution had for Bernstein.

The continuity between Adenauer's and Brandt's foreign policy is underlined by Brandt's complaint(made during the 1965 election campaign, which he fought as leader of the opposition), that the Federal Republic was 'an economic giant but a political dwarf': as Chancellor four years later, he was to show how he intended to bring West Germany's political status up to her economic one. The conduct of the *Ostpolitik* itself entailed, as we have seen, some very determined, skilful, and well-planned diplomatic activity, worked out with a strategic foresight unmatched by any previous government of the Federal Republic. The contrast is particularly clear if Brandt's pursuit of *Ostpolitik* as Chancellor between 1969 and 1973 is compared with his efforts in the same direction during his period as Foreign Minister under the Grand Coalition (1966–69). During the earlier period, the Cabinet were very clearly divided on the issue of how to deal with the East: the CDU, in particular, had strong inhibitions about dealing with either Moscow or East Berlin. This meant that the Grand Coalition's *Ostpolitik* was limited mainly to a series of pragmatic approaches to the 'middle layer' of the Socialist bloc, by-passing the GDR, ignoring Moscow, and concentrating on the 'easy' countries, Romania and Yugoslavia. The dangers of this policy, and the very limited nature of its potential results, were clearly indicated by the Soviet invasion of Czechoslovakia in August 1968: part of the immediate background to this tragedy, and part of the Soviet justification for military intervention, was that the West German government, having established diplomatic relations with Bucharest and Belgrade during 1967, was now actively turning its attention to Prague. It would of course be ludicrous to say that the Soviet intervention in Czechoslovakia was in any sense a reasonable or justifiable response to 'revanchist' German designs, but August 1968 showed the bankruptcy of Bonn's policy of pressing forward with bilateral economic and diplomatic dealings with the countries of Eastern Europe without making the overall political objectives clear.

After Brandt's accession to the Chancellorship at the end of 1969, he resumed the *Ostpolitik,* defining its overall objectives much more clearly. Besides emphasising the Federal Republic's deep-seated commitment to the West — for instance, by his active diplomacy at the Hague summit conference of the EEC in December 1969 — he took great care to underline the non-offensive character of his *Ostpolitik* and thus reassure both Moscow and East Berlin, the two Eastern capitals that had been left out of the previous West German government's pragmatic attempts at *Ostpolitik.*

Brandt's meetings with the East German head of government, Willi Stoph, at Erfurt and Kassel, and his visits to Moscow and Warsaw,

underlined the commitments his government was making in the negotiations themselves: to extend formal recognition to the GDR, and to seek
reconciliation with Poland and the Soviet Union through accepting the
Oder-Neisse Line. The Bonn government's conduct of the negotiations
reflected this overall strategic concept; and, during 1970, interrelated
negotiations were carried out with Moscow, Warsaw and East Berlin.

The dynamic element in this policy, and the fact that it emanated from
a German state with a new sense of self-confidence, caused some concern
on the part of Allies. Even though they were in agreement with the
general substance of the *Ostpolitik* — which after all represented the
policy of *détente* they had themselves been pursuing in varying ways for a
number of years — they were somewhat taken aback to find a West
German government acting with such despatch and with such self-
assurance, and, above all, without full preliminary consultations with
them. The *Ostpolitik* was dynamic both in its substance and in its
implications: by the mid-1970s, West German policy was to deal with the
Western world with the same kind of self-assurance it has shown in dealing
with the Eastern world at the beginning of the decade.

The central question facing any observer of the Federal Republic's
foreign policy is the one that the veteran philosopher Karl Jaspers posed
in 1966: 'where is the Federal Republic heading?'[1] In the mid-1960s,
before the decisive breakthrough of Brandt's *Ostpolitik,* the answer was
that the Federal Republic was in effect driving itself into a blind alley,
through its insistence on the totally unrealistic goal of territorial
reunification. Due to West Germany's acceptance of the division of
Germany, and the consequent establishment of the Federal Republic as an
autonomous actor on the world scene, the answer is now much more
open. The critics of Brandt's *Ostpolitik* have argued — and this criticism
has been a substantial factor in party politics in West Germany — that the
Ostpolitik implied the Federal Republic's turning its back on the West,
and that Brandt, Bahr, and the other politicians responsible for this policy
were endangering the solidarity of the European Community and NATO
in the interests of something approaching a new Rapallo Treaty with the
East. Although this line of criticism was by no means followed by the
CDU/CSU opposition as a whole, it was given some encouragement by the
circumstance that the fiftieth anniversary of Rapallo occurred in the
spring of 1972, just at the height of the controversy over *Ostpolitik.*
Certain critics with an exaggerated sense of the historical parallels involved
attempted to maintain that the *Ostpolitik* represented something in the
nature of a new 'Rapallo policy' — in other words, that the Federal
Republic's foreign policy was tending towards a revival of the alignment

with the Soviet Union reached in 1922. In fact, Egon Bahr — though his Berlin background had certainly made him more sceptical of West European integration than he might have been had he, like Adenauer, been a Rhinelander — came nowhere near pursuing such a policy. This did not, however, prevent his more extreme critics, in and around the CDU, from arguing that the *Ostpolitik* was reorientating the Federal Republic towards the East, and that the Western Alliance was being destroyed and diluted in the process. An article by Walter Hahn, in which the author draws on a confidential interview that Bahr granted him in 1969, provides an example of such criticism. Leaving aside the issue of the propriety of publishing an interview originally given in confidence, one notes that Bahr is presented in this article as a man bent on downgrading the importance of the European Community and NATO as elements in West Germany's foreign policy, in order that a pan-European security system, in which the two Germanies — demilitarised and neutralised — would coexist under a loose guarantee provided by the Western powers and the Soviet Union, could be set up.[2] This scenario, which was presumably sketched out by Bahr in his 1969 capacity as a foreign policy planner concerned with evolving hypothetical futures, is most unlikely to have corresponded either to the short-term, or even to the long-term, intentions of the Brandt government: it is however, worth recording here, as an example of the intentions attributed to Brandt by his Right-wing critics — particularly as the Springer Press, having foreknowledge of the article, exploited to the maximum its value as propaganda.

Some of *Ostpolitik's* defenders in the West, and particularly Germans concerned to defend Brandt's intentions *vis-à-vis* his Western allies, seem to have gone almost as far in the opposite direction, by making the paradoxical assertion that the co-effect of *Ostpolitik* has been to tie the Federal Republic more closely than ever to the West. Not only, they argued, did *Ostpolitik* have a firm base in *Westpolitik*, in the sense that West Germany remained a most loyal and active member of NATO and the European Community, but it also contributed to *Westpolitik*, in the sense that it was only by renouncing the aim of German reunification that the Federal Republic became a fully-committed member of the West European community. If the EEC were seriously to attempt to transform itself into a political union by 1980, then the West Germans had a particular responsibility to rid themselves of the encumbering legacy of their national past, and to prepare themselves to take the Federal Republic into this union on the same terms as the other states of Western Europe. *Ostpolitik,* according to this argument, had the effect of giving the Federal Republic the same position — as France, Belgium, or the

United Kingdom — that of an essentially West European state. The normalisation of relations between the two German states meant that West Germany's relations with the GDR would, in reality, not be too different from, say, the UK's relations with Poland or France's relations with Czechoslovakia, and the West Germans would therefore be able to take part wholeheartedly in the process of political unification in Western Europe.[3]

This argument, while not exaggerated to the same degree as the contrary thesis, which views the *Ostpolitik* as a 'new Rapallo', clearly goes too far — at least in the sharp formulatiom just outlined. To realise this, one has only to recall Brandt's clear commitment to preserving the 'substance of the German nation', and Bonn's insistence that recognition of the political division of Germany does not entail recognition of the GDR as a foreign country. The truth lies, as is so often the case, between the two extremes. *Ostpolitik* has indeed been firmly based on *Westpolitik* in the sense that there has been no intention of deflecting the Federal Republic from its Western alignment and bringing more in line with the East, and little risk of this occurring accidentally. On the other hand, the argument that *Ostpolitik* amounts to no more than the redefinition of the Federal Republic's true character as a West European state is also exaggerated, because it takes no account of the continuing German commitment to Berlin and the continuing concern for the population of the GDR — a factor that gives a unique character to the Federal Republic's relationship with the East.

We thus return to the central question: if reunification as a goal of foreign policy had been abandoned — and *Ostpolitik* means the recognition or acceptance of the territorial *status quo* in Europe, including the division of Germany into two states — what can the Federal Republic do through its foreign policy that it could not do before? There are, of course, a number of general objectives that the Federal Republic must have in common with Britain and France: for instance, the promotion of its people's economic prosperity and well-being, despite the difficulties created by world inflation and the threatened shortage of energy. Again the Federal Republic, like other medium powers, will be concerned with the less tangible goals of its political status and influence in the international system. The analysis of its foreign policy, however, will require us to go more deeply into the question of precisely what content has been put into these general objectives by those in authority. This in turn requires some consideration of the nature of the international system of the 1970s and the kinds of objectives that this system will permit its medium-sized members to pursue. The question of whether, for example, the Federal Republic is likely to adopt any foreign policy remotely resembling a 'new Rapallo' requires us to consider whether the international system of today is in any way comparable to that of the 1920s. A contrast between the 1970s and the 1920s in this respect will also, more generally, indicate what sort of limits are set to West German foreign policy objectives by the Federal Republic's external environment.

The international system of the inter-war years may be said to differ in at least three important respects from that of the present day. First, this system — which formed the context of German foreign policy from the Treaty of Versailles in 1919 to the war against Poland in 1939 — was one in which the various national units were in a real sense sovereign. Even though sovereignty may in legal terms be absolute, political realities determine that some states are more sovereign than others; and the nature of international relations between the wars was marked by the fact that several states possessed really effective sovereignty. Despite the web of war debts and reparation payments, and other links that rendered states interdependent, most of them were in real terms more sovereign than are most states today.

Secondly, the system was a multipolar one, in the sense that there were a large number of centres of power, and as a result, the politics of Europe, if not the politics of the world, were subject to influences from a considerable number of sources. Such states as Germany, France, Britain and Italy all counted for a good deal in the system, while the Soviet Union and the United States were only marginally involved in the great issues of international relations. It is, of course, true that the United States played an important part in economic diplomacy, and the Soviet Union was very active on the sidelines (the Rapallo Treaty of 1922 is evidence of that), but the diffusion of effective freedom of action away from the two future super-powers was very marked.

The third main feature of the inter-war system resulted from the combination of the first two: the effective sovereignty of medium-sized units, combined with their multiplicity, meant that the states of the period were able to be very flexible in their choice of international alignments. If one thinks of the degree to which Britain and France came together, then diverged, then attempted to come together again during the 1920s and 1930s, and if one thinks of the way in which Germany swung from trying to renegotiate the Treaty of Versailles in 1921 towards alignment with the Soviet Union in 1922 (the Rapallo Treaty), then back towards the West in 1925 (Locarno), then again towards Moscow in 1926, the degree of flexibility and unpredictability in the system is very clear. (This same point is confirmed by the changeability of Italian foreign policy under Mussolini: assent to the Locarno Pact in 1925 (supposed to guarantee the *status quo*) was followed by a unilateral breach of the peace in Abyssinia ten years later, and then by the Axis alignment with Hitler.) In such a system, Germany, with her central geographical position and her large economic resources, could and did — despite the shackles of the Treaty of Versailles — play an independent and, at times, disturbing role.

The degree of independence enjoyed by states in the inter-war period is underlined by briefly comparing it to the situation in the international system of the 1950s, when Cold-War bipolarity was at its height. All three variables identified as characterising the inter-war period had been translated into their extreme opposites. First, the sovereignty of most states has been drastically curtailed — not only by the military balance of power, but also by a considerable increase in interdependence, reflected in the institutions of European economic integration; secondly, the two super-powers dominated a distinctly bipolar system, which stood in direct contrast to the multipolarity of the inter-war years; and, thirdly, this situation sharply reduced, for most states, the degree to which they could be flexible about their alignments. The Federal Republic's foreign policy under Adenauer was particularly marked by this inflexibility, as shown for instance by the Hallstein Doctrine adopted in 1956; by this the Federal Republic forswore diplomatic relations with any state that recognised the GDR (with the one, sensible exception of the Soviet Union). While this is, perhaps, an extreme example of diplomatic inflexibility, it does illustrate how immobile German foreign policy was during this period, and how greatly it contrasted with Germany's policy in the 1920s.

More broadly, the 1950s was characterised by a situation in which the Western powers concentrated essentially on building up NATO, the European Community, and other organisations demonstrating Western solidarity, while the Eastern states concentrated their efforts on relations within the Warsaw Pact and Comecon. There was thus very little interaction between the two systems, offering another striking contrast to the flexibility of alignment that we have detected in the inter-war period. In this situation, Adenauer made the very clear choice to build up West Germany's relations with the Western world, refusing to be tempted into diplomatic involvement with the East.

If we now turn our attention from the 1950s to the 1970s, the question arises of how the international context of West Germany's foreign policy has changed. In some ways the situation in the 1970s is clearly very different from that in the 1950s. Even though economic interdependence has, if anything, increased, so that the freedom of action of individual states — even large and powerful ones — is still markedly less than it was in the 1920s and 1930s, it is clear that some of them have recovered that freedom to at least some degree. Despite all the limitations on the effective sovereignty of West European states (their economic dependence on imported oil, for instance), it is hard to argue that the international system of today is as lacking in flexibility as that of the 1950s. The two super-powers do, of course, remain pre-eminent in some ways, but a world in which they undertake negotiations on strategic weapons. on economic transactions, and on other matters, is without doubt a different one from that of the Cold-War confrontation. The mere fact that intensive negotiations between the two blocs are now taking place (both major negotiations on strategic matters, and a wide variety of bilateral dealings are under way) is a reminder that the inflexibilities of the 1950s have been in large measure overcome. The effective limits on the independent freedom of action of medium powers have been illustrated by the failure both of de Gaulle and of Brandt to bring about *fundamental* changes in the system as a whole, though the fact that these powers can attempt such foreign policies confirms that a good deal has changed.

In the context of these international developments, we can return to the questions of how much freedom of action the Federal Republic is now in fact likely to enjoy, and what its foreign policy concerns are likely to be in the new situation. As we have already suggested, Bonn's foreign policy is likely to contain elements both of *Ostpolitik* and of *Westpolitik.* It is, however, clear that, during the second half of the 1970s, *Ostpolitik* will be a more multilateral affair than it was during the dramatic breakthrough of the Brandt period. There is a good deal of truth in the agrument that West Germany will now become a 'normal' member of the West European community of states, and will co-ordinate its role with that of its West European partners in such East—West discussions as the remaining stages of the Conference on Security and Co-operation in Europe. It is also true that in the continuing East—West negotiations on arms control — the discussions of Mutual and Balanced Force Reductions — West Germany's position will be closely co-ordinated with that of its Western allies. It is even likely that, as the process of East—West co-operation develops, West Germany will act in harmony with its EEC partners, rather than bilaterally with its Eastern interlocutors, on an increasing number of economic issues involving the East. At the same time, one should not forget the special position of the Federal Republic *vis-à-vis* the GDR, so that, for instance, the special provisions governing trade between the two states are likely to remain intact. In essence, these arrangements mean that West Germany pays a considerable price financially for the symbolic gesture of keeping alive the unity of the

German nation. Again, certain concerns of *Ostpolitik* − notably the position of Berlin − will mean a good deal more to the Federal Republic than to its Western partners.

Together with these specifically 'Eastern' concerns, however, there remains the fact that the improvement of the Federal Republic's relations with the East has in a number of ways altered her standing, and improved her relative power position in the West. In both NATO and the European Community, the Federal Republic is now in a position to press its own interests much more firmly than in the days before if recognised the GDR and formally renounced its territorial claims in the East. Even though, as we have noted, West German spokesmen from Adenauer onwards have always been ready to stand up for the Federal Republic's national interests, and have done so effectively, there were many occasions during the 1950s and 1960s when these interests were allowed to take second place to Western solidarity. The Federal Republic simply did not feel in a position to resist American demands for payment of a higher proportion of the cost of stationing American troops in Europe, or French demands for price increases under the Common Agricultural Policy. From now on, West Germany's relations with its partners will − as shown in the EEC negotiations of 1973 and 1974 − be marked by a firmer assertion of its own interests. Even though the Federal Republic has a very clear interest in keeping substantial numbers of American troops in Europe − an interest of which Chancellor Schmidt, as a former Defence Minister, is very well aware − the German posture in offset negotiations is likely to be firmer; again, although West Germany has a strong interest in the continuation of the EEC, seeing it as an essential market for its exports, and will therefore continue to make certain concessions on agricultural matters, these concessions will be made more reluctantly than in the past. The same attitude will be shown towards other proposals for Community spending that require a large financial outlay from the Federal Republic − for instance, the proposed regional and social policies.

West German attitudes towards the EEC have changed partly because of the changes in the Community as a whole. In 1973, while Heath and Pompidou were still in power and committed to the development of the Community towards a 'European union', it was logical for Brandt to argue that Germany would be in a position to increase her financial contributions only if her partners took active steps towards developing the institutions of the Community in the direction of what he called a 'European government'. In 1974, with both Wilson and Giscard d'Estaing adopting markedly more pragmatic attitudes towards Europe − in effect turning the Community into a loose-knit intergovernmental structure with very few supranational pretensions — it is logical for Schmidt to retreat from the outspokenly 'European' convictions of his predecessor.

It would be going much too far to say that the Federal Republic under Chancellor Schmidt is completely turning its back on the idea of European integration. While still Minister for European Affairs in the Brandt government, Hans Apel, (now Schmidt's Minister of Finance), confirmed West Germany's wish to strengthen the institutions of the Community by moving towards majority voting in the Council of Ministers, upgrading the powers of the European Parliament, and so on.[4] It is however, clear, from the general attitude of the Schmidt government towards its European partners that they will have to count on a more self-reliant and independent attitude from West Germany than they were used to in the past. It has been seen that one of the most important reasons for this development was Brandt's successful pursuit of *Ostpolitik*. It should again be emphasised that this recovery of power and independence by the Federal Republic is most unlikely to portend a return to anything remotely resembling the degree of independence 'enjoyed' by the Weimar Republic in the 1920s or the Third Reich in the 1930s. Our survey of the principal differences between the international systems of the inter-war years and the 1970s has confirmed that the possibilities open to even a relatively strong 'medium power' like West Germany are vastly more limited than they were. However, what we are likely to witness is a reassertion of the Federal Republic's importance as the leading member of the European Community and as the principal Western partner of the United States. *Ostpolitik* will continue to be pursued along the lines indicated above. It is even possible that there will be some symbolic gesture of Socialist fraternity between the SPD and SED, to mark the centenary of the Gotha Congress of May 1875, the moment when unity was achieved between the rival German Socialist parties of a century ago; but the serious concerns of the Federal Republic's external relations will continue to lie essentially with the West.

Notes

[1] Karl Jaspers, *Wohin Treibt die Bundesrepublik: Tatsachen, Gefahren, Chancen,* Munich 1966.

[2] Walter Hahn, 'West Germany's Ostpolitik: the Grand Design of Egon Bahr' in *Orbis* vol. 16, no. 4, Winter 1973.

[3] This argument is advanced, for instance, at the end of a penetrating article by Christoph Bertram, 'West German perspectives on European

security: continuity and change' in *The World Today,* March 1971.

⁴ Hans Apel, 'Europa am Scheideweg' in *Europa-Archiv* vol. 29, no. 4, 25 February 1974.

Index

110

Schnitzer, Martin 67, 74, 75
Schollwer 33
Schröder, Gerhard 34, 37, 50
Schulz, E. 30, 42
Schulz, Eberhard and Hans Dieter 75
Schumacher, Kurt 27
Schwarz, Hans-Peter 14, 21
SED (Socialist Unity Party) 9, 10, 14, 61–71, 88–9, 107
Seebohm, H.C. 33
Sindermann, Horst 62–3
Smith, Jean Edward 73
Social Democratic Party, *see* SPD
Socialist Unity Party, *see* SED
Solzhenitsyn, Alexander 65
Sommer, Theo. 36, 43, 73
Sontheimer, Kurt 7, 15, 21, 22, 24, 42
SPD (Social Democratic Party) 1, 2, 5, 11–12, 14, 26–8, 29, 32–4, 37–9, 45–6, 89, 107; *see also* SPD/FDP coalition
SPD/FDP coalition 47, 71, 81, 85
Springer Press 32, 35, 101
SRP (Neo-nazi party) 27
Stalin, Joseph 60
Steed, R.H.C. 88, 93
Stern, Carola 73
Stockhausen, Karlheinz 25
Stolper, W.F. 73
Stoph, Willi 35, 61–3, 81–2, 99
Strauss, Franz-Josef 46, 50, 54–5, 98

Stücklen, Richard 54

Thalheim, K.C. 73
Thälmann, Ernst 68–9
Thiele, H.J. 43
Tilford, Roger 1–21

Ulbricht, Walter 31, 60–2, 65, 68, 73

Verner, Paul 61

Walser, Martin 50
Warnecke, Stephen 28
Warneke, Lothar 70
Warnke, Herbert 62
Webb, W.L. 69, 74
Weber, Hermann 73
Wehner, Herbert 27, 71
Weizsäcker, Richard von 51
Whetton, L. 80, 92
Wilson, Harold 106
Wrangel, Olaf von 37
Writers' Congress (7th) 70

Young Union (CDU's youth movement) 51

Zauberman, A. 73
Ziebura, G. 29, 42
Zundel, Rolf 43

111